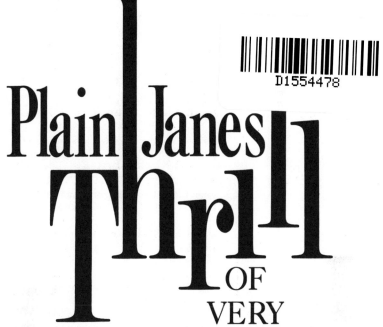

Plain Janes Thrill

OF VERY FATTENING FOODS COOKBOOK

By
Linda Sunshine

Illustrations by Alison Seiffer

Designed by Larry Kazal

St. Martin's Press
New York

In memory of my father,
Dr. Harold K. Sunshine

Plain Jane is a trademark of Linda Sunshine.

Recipes for Crushed Ice Cream Cone Pie, Peanut Brittle Fudge Squares, Grasshopper Pie, Turtle Pie, and Chocolate Peanut Butter Cheesecake are reprinted with permission of The Baskin-Robbins Ice Cream Company.

Hershey Bar Pie, Easy Peanut Butter Fudge, and Reese's Pieces Ice Cream Saucers are reprinted with permission of The Hershey Company.

Milky Way Cake, Heath Bar Cake, and Pink Lemonade Pie are reprinted from *The Chosen: Appetizers and Desserts* by Marilyn Stone, © 1982. Available from Triad Publishing Company, 1110 NW 8th Avenue, Gainesville, Florida 32601. Send $8.95 (paper) or $11.95 (spiral) and $1.50 postage.

Chocolate/Potato Chip cookie recipe from *The 47 Best Chocolate Chip Cookies in the World*. Reprinted with permission of St. Martin's Press.

Every attempt has been made to properly credit recipes to their original sources. If I've inadvertently miscredited a recipe, please write to me, in care of St. Martin's Press, 175 Fifth Avenue, N.Y., N.Y. 10010, and I will correct the error in subsequent printings of the book.

ISBN: 0-312-613-822

First Edition
10 9 8 7 6 5 4 3 2 1

Dedicated to Phil Donahue, Jane Pauley, Diane Sawyer, David Hartman, Johnny Carson, David Letterman, and anyone else who might possibly promote this book on national television.

Contents

Introduction

IN my last book, *Plain Jane Works Out*, I carefully explained my daily exercise program. Even though others tried to duplicate my success, they could not touch the loyalty of my audience or hurt the sales of my book. Clearly, the public saw that I had more to offer than Victoria Principal or Linda Evans (about fifty pounds more, to be precise).

Today, women (and men) all across the country (and in seven foreign languages, too) are doing The Refrigerator Lunge, as I instructed, at least a dozen times a day.

I couldn't be more delighted! But, I want to caution my readers: Exercise alone will not keep you fifteen pounds overweight (at least not on a permanent basis). For that added bonus, you will need a steady diet of fattening foods.

My readers understand the importance of diet and nutrition. As I tour the country to promote myself (and my book), people constantly ask me about nutrition. "Plain Jane," they'll say, "after I bought your book [and several additional copies for my friends and relatives] I went home and did The Refrigerator Lunge. But, now I need to know, what's to eat in the refrigerator?"

Or, they'll want to know: "Plain Jane, what do you recommend after a strenuous workout? Twinkies or Devil Dogs?"

These are, of course, serious considerations. A truly well-balanced diet plan should include *both* Twinkies *and* Devil Dogs.

As I said before (and I'll say it again): The simple fact is that exercise alone just isn't enough. You need to eat the proper foods and Plain Jane is here to give you all the high-calorie recipes you'll ever need. (Who better for the job?)

In the following pages, you will find the recipes I have collected over the years. These represent my favorite fattening foods. In addition,

I have fleshed out (to coin a phrase) my recipes with recipes from friends, relatives, business associates, and the woman who sat next to me on the train last Thursday. Most importantly, however, I have included recipes from my mother's kitchen where I first learned to cook every dish with heavy cream, sour cream, or cream cheese.

In *Plain Jane's Thrill of Very Fattening Foods Cookbook*, I'll cover the three most important meals of the day: Desserts, Appetizers, and Snacks. And then I'll include a few recipes for the lesser courses: Entrees, Side Dishes, and Take-Out.

If you are looking for fresh vegetables or garden salads, look elsewhere. The only salads I ever recommended are potato and macaroni (together).

In these pages, I celebrate the infamous words of the Duchess of Windsor.*

Known throughout the world as the toast of high society and quoted in every chic magazine, the Duchess is best remembered for once having said: "Darling, food can never be too rich or too fattening."

So, if by using the recipes in this book, your meals turn out to be too rich or too fattening, then, darling, please, be sure to invite me and the Duchess over for dinner.

Plain Jane

Blimpie's Restaurant
New York City
June, 1984

*That's Windsor, Rhode Island, where the Duchess attended Vocational High School.

Desserts

WHEN planning a dinner party, the first step is to select your dessert because desserts are the most crucial part of any meal. No one would argue that desserts can make or break a meal (no one that I know, at least).

Here are two important tips when planning for this crucial course:

1) Do not repeat ingredients from course to course. If, for instance, you decide to serve Brownie Ice Cream Loaf for dessert (recipe on pg. 57), do *not* serve Chicken in Chocolate Mole Sauce for an entree (Chicken in Chocolate Mole Sauce should only be served with a contrasting dessert such as White Chocolate Mousse (recipe on pg. 48).

2) Always be prepared for an emergency. Keep your pantry well stocked with the basics for survival: confectioner's sugar, condensed milk, graham cracker crusts, and Marshmallow Fluff.

The recipes in this chapter have been carefully selected for their taste, quality, and high-calorie content. Almost all of these recipes are made with ingredients that are either chemical, alcohol, or cholesterol but, then, that's why they all taste so darned good.

My Mom's Incredibly Fattening Noodle Pudding

Pam's Mom's Noodle Pudding with Apricots

No-bake Ice Box Cake

Rebel Yell 15,000 Calorie Cake

Galliano Cake

Milky Way Cake

Heath Bar Cake

Thomas Anderson's Favorite Chocolate-
chocolate-chip Cake

Mimi's Triple Layer Chocolate Cake

Plain Jane Carrot Cake

The Bestest Brownies

Sandra's Mother's Frozen Chocolate Velvet Pie

Chocolate Mousse Pie

Susie's Pink Lemonade Pie

Hershey Bar Pie

Brandy Alexander Pie

Rich Rhubarb Cream Pie

Susan's Roommate-From-College's Frozen
Yogurt Pie

M&M Cookies

Chocolate Chip/Potato Chip Cookies

Doug's Cookies

Almond Crescent Cookies

Grandmother Avignone's Zabaglione

Jello Trifle Supreme

Lynn's Amaretto Mold

Ann's Amaretti Cream Topping

Pudding by Mr. Tux

Susan's Toblerone Mousse

Flo's Cool-Whip Mousse

White Chocolate Mousse with Strawberry Sauce
in Tuiles Shells

Fattening Fruit Salad

My Sister's Apple Crisp

Adam's Apples and Peanut Butter

Chocolate Peanut Butter Cheesecake

Junior's Famous Cheesecake

Cooking with Ice Cream

Peanut Brittle Fudge Squares

Crushed Ice Cream Cone Pie

Grasshopper Pie

Turtle Pie

Brownie Ice Cream Loaf

Reese's Pieces Ice Cream Saucers

Banana Flambé

Candy Cooking

The Chocolate-Dipped Calvin Klein Strawberry

Lindsey's Bourbon Balls

Marshmallow Fluff Fudge

Easy Peanut Butter Fudge

Aunt Mitzi's Chocolate-Peanut Delights

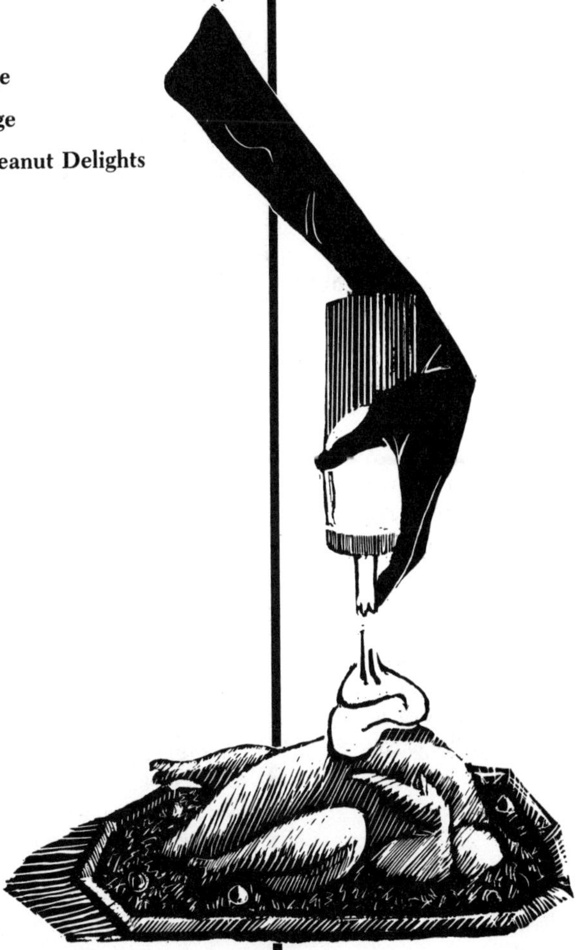

My Mom's Incredibly Fattening Noodle Pudding

THERE are two heirlooms in my family: Nana Sunshine's hand-crocheted tablecloth and my Mom's noodle pudding. I'll never part with Nana's tablecloth but, for the sake of my royalty account, I'm willing to surrender my mother's recipe.

Let me warn you, this is no ordinary noodle pudding. Forget the bland puddings of your past. My Mom's noodle pudding tastes exactly like cheesecake. (It should—it's every bit as fattening.) Listen, I was raised on this noodle concoction and the proof of the pudding is right here on my thighs.

Serve this pudding warm, as a side dish with brisket, pot roast, roast beef, chicken, or turkey. (It's like having dessert *with* the main course.) Serve it as a dessert with fruit and coffee. Serve it as lunch for finicky kids. Better yet, forget the brisket, forget the turkey, forget the fruit and coffee, forget the kids—grab a fork and serve yourself.

INGREDIENTS

When shopping at Dunkin' Donuts, pretend you are the mother of nine. Say things like, "Little David likes cream-filled and Susie wanted jelly." That way, no one will be suspicious when you order a dozen donuts with one cup of coffee to go.

1 *pound noodles*
4 *ounces butter*
1 *cup sugar*
4 *eggs*
½ *pound cottage cheese, pot style (Don't panic—you'll never taste the cottage cheese)*
1 *pint sour cream*
2 *apples (peeled, cored, cut up)*
1 *small can of peaches (drain syrup)*
1 *teaspoon vanilla*
½ *jar orange marmalade*
½ *cup raisins*
1 *pint milk*
½ *cup cornflakes*
2 *tablespoons cinnamon sugar*

1. Preheat oven to 350°.
2. Parboil noodles (5 minutes) in 4 quarts of salted water and drain.
3. Melt butter over noodles, making sure all noodles are drenched in butter.
4. Mix sugar and eggs with electric blender. Add cheese, sour cream, and milk.

5. Fold in apples, peaches, vanilla, marmalade, and raisins.
6. Add mixture to noodles.
7. Pour everything into a large glass baking dish. Fill dish ¾ to rim—allow space for pudding to rise.
8. Lightly sprinkle crushed cornflakes over top of pudding. Dot with butter and cinnamon sugar.
9. Bake at 350° for one hour.

This pudding can easily be frozen and reheated in case of such emergencies as unexpected company, working late, forgetting to stop at the grocery store, Monday morning, Saturday night, Tuesday afternoon, a sports event on television, or any month spelled with three or more letters.

Pam's Mom's Noodle Pudding with Apricots

SORRY Mom, but Pam's Mom also makes a pretty mean noodle pudding.

Now, it's true that my mother's noodle pudding is better than Pam's Mom's noodle pudding, *but* in the name of fair play and democratic kitchens, I am presenting both recipes so that my readers can make their own choice.

INGREDIENTS

½ *pound wide noodles*
1 8-ounce package cream cheese
¼ *cup milk*
1 pound cottage cheese
½ *pint sour cream*
¼ *cup sugar*
½ *cup dried apricots (quartered)*
¼ *pound melted butter*
5 or 6 eggs
1 teaspoon vanilla

Topping:
8 ounces cornflakes
¼ *pound butter, melted*
1 cup brown sugar

1. Preheat oven to 350°.
2. Cook noodles in boiling, salted water. Drain

and rinse under cold water.

3. Mash cream cheese with milk.

4. Put drained noodles in a bowl and add all the ingredients (except for topping ingredients).

5. Butter an oblong baking dish and pour in noodle mixture.

6. Crumble cornflakes. Add brown sugar and melted butter and mix well.

7. Spread topping over noodles.

8. Bake in a preheated 350° oven for 40 minutes.

Serves 8.

THE TEN MOST-OFTEN-ASKED CULINARY QUESTIONS

1. What's for dinner?

2. When are we eating?

3. Did you go food shopping today?

4. Isn't there *anything* to eat in this house?

5. Do I have to eat this?

6. Do you smell something burning?

7. Can I have my dessert now?

8. Are we out of milk *again?*

9. Where's the ketchup?

10. Can't we eat out tonight?

Dear Plain Jane,

I gain weight just by looking at food. What can I do?

Irma S.
Biloxi, Miss.

Dear Irma,

Close your eyes.

Wear dark glasses.

Get a seeing eye dog and let him gain the weight for you.

Jane

No-bake Ice Box Cake

ICEBOX cake was invented during the 1940s when there was a shortage of flour and sugar. That, at least, is the legend behind this cake. Personally, I think it was invented by someone with an Oreo Complex (which you'll understand in a moment).

If you like whipped cream (and you'd better if you want to talk to me), this is the cake for you. It's also one of the few instances where the preparation is as fattening as the cake. Be sure to carefully read and follow these directions *exactly* as written.

INGREDIENTS

2 cups heavy cream
4 tablespoons sugar
1 teaspoon vanilla extract
1 box NABISCO FAMOUS CHOCOLATE WAFERS (Substitutes will not do. If you can't find Nabisco Famous, find a bakery or a box of Twinkies but forget about making this cake with anything other than Nabisco Famous Chocolate Wafers.)

1. Pour cream into the bowl. (It will be easier to whip the cream if the bowl is chilled.) Add sugar and vanilla. Whip with electric mixer or whisk until cream swirls and peaks.

2. Using your pointer finger, scoop a dollop of whipped cream into your mouth and say "Yum!" Repeat twice.

3. Spread one wafer with cream. Cover with another wafer—like a sandwich. Make a stack of four wafer sandwiches. Top the last with cream.

4. Repeat Step #2.

5. Repeat Step #4.

6. Stand the stack of wafers on its side. Add another stack of four to the first stack until the row has 16 wafers.

7. Repeat Step #2. Lick the whipped cream off the whisk or the beaters of your electric mixer. (Important reminder: Make sure the electric mixer is OFF when you attempt this.)

8. Make another row of wafers, putting it next to the first row.

9. Lick the spatula.

10. Frost the outside of the stacks with remaining cream.

11. Repeat Step #9.

12. Refrigerate the cake for at least 3 hours.

13. Clean up by licking the bowl, the spoon, your apron, and the kitchen table.
14. To serve, slice diagonally from one side to the other.

Rebel Yell 15,000 Calorie Cake

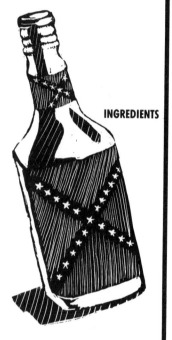

FOR all you unsuspecting cooks, Rebel Yell is Southern bourbon and you use lots of it in this recipe. (I think the bourbon is to wash down the pound of macaroons and dozen eggs.)

Rebel Yell Cake was concocted by Sigrid Burton Brennan's grandmother. My friend Jean says that you take one bite of this cake and your teeth start to hurt.

This is, without question, the single-most fattening recipe in this cookbook, perhaps in any cookbook. And I must warn you to prepare yourself before you read the list of ingredients. Those of you without a serious sweet tooth may find the following list difficult, if not fatal, to review. It's best read with a bottle of smelling salts close at hand.

INGREDIENTS

(get ready):
1 pound Italian macaroons, broken
1 cup Rebel Yell (or other brand) bourbon
2 cups butter
½ cup sugar
½ cup confectioner's sugar
1 dozen eggs (separated)
4 ounces unsweetened chocolate, melted
1 teaspoon vanilla
1 cup chopped pecans
1 dozen ladyfinger cakes, opened into 24 pieces
Whipped cream

1. Have a cocktail while you soak the macaroons in the bourbon.
2. Cream butter and sugars.
3. Beat in egg yolks and then melted chocolate.
4. Add vanilla and chopped pecans.
5. Beat egg whites silly (until stiff) and then fold into chocolate mixture.
6. Line ladyfingers around the sides of a spring-form pan.
7. Cover bottom of pan with one layer of soaked macaroons.
8. Make another layer of chocolate mixture.
9. Alternate layers until you've used all of the macaroons and the chocolate mixture.
10. Chill overnight.

11. To serve, remove sides of the pan and cover the top of the cake with a thick layer of whipped cream.

I do believe, Miss Scarlett, this cake may be the reason the South lost the war!

IF you've ever baked a cake from scratch, you know that it involves a lot of time and effort. Generally, my rule of thumb is that I only bake a scratch cake when I have absolutely nothing else to do. Otherwise, I bake a Galliano cake, which is every bit as good as most, and much better than some, scratch cakes.

This has got to be the simplest recipe in the world. I mean, it's easier to bake this cake than it is to shop at a bakery (when you include the time it takes to get into the car, drive to the bakery, take a number, select a cake(s), sample the freebies and drive home—not to mention the time spent dressing the baby or searching for your keys). By comparison, you can prepare Galliano Cake in just under 4 minutes 37 seconds (depending on how fast you can crack an egg).

1 box Duncan Hines Deluxe Yellow Cake Mix
1 box instant vanilla pudding
1 cup Wesson Oil
¾ cup orange juice
4 eggs
¼ – ½ cup Galliano (or buy those sample "airplane" bottles from your local liquor store)

1. Preheat oven to 325°.
2. Mix together all ingredients.
3. Pour batter into a greased bundt pan.
4. Bake at 325° for 45 to 50 minutes.
5. Allow to cool before removing from pan.
6. Sprinkle with powdered sugar.

To make this cake even more fattening, you can either eat the whole thing yourself or serve it topped with your favorite flavor ice cream and/or Fattening Fruit Salad (recipe on pg. 50).

Galliano Cake

INGREDIENTS

Milky Way Cake

INGREDIENTS

SEE if you can correctly answer the following Multiple Choice Question:

What is the single-most perfect food substance in the world?

a) wheat
b) rice
c) soybean
d) barley
e) Milky Way candy bars

Now, honestly, how many of you really knew that the right answer was *e)* Milky Way candy bars?

My more intelligent readers know that, by definition, the perfect food substance is edible in every conceivable form and only Milky Ways fit this criterion. Milky Ways are delicious frozen and, yet, they can also be eaten raw. (Can the same be said for barley?) Melted, like at the beach, Milky Ways are gooey but still divine. And, as proven with the following recipe, Milky Ways are absolutely scrumptious when consumed in cake form.

Yes, the Milky Way bar is truly a universal food stuff, which is probably the reason why they named an entire solar system for this humble candy bar.

6 *Milky Way candy bars for the cake*
1 *Milky Way candy bar for the cook*
1 *cup (2 sticks) sweet butter*
2 *cups sugar*
4 *eggs*
2½ *cups flour, sifted*
½ *teaspoon baking soda*
1¼ *cups buttermilk*
1 *teaspoon vanilla*
1 *cup chopped nuts (optional)*

1. Melt six Milky Ways and ½ cup (1 stick) butter in a saucepan over a very low heat. Set aside. Eat the seventh Milky Way yourself while you preheat oven to 350°.
2. Beat sugar and remaining butter until fluffy.
3. Add eggs, one at a time, beating well after each addition.

4. Add flour and baking soda alternately with buttermilk, stirring until smooth.
5. Add candy mixture, stirring well.
6. Stir in vanilla and nuts.
7. Pour into greased, floured bundt pan.
8. Bake at 350° for 1 hour and 15 to 25 minutes (test with toothpick).
9. Cool in pan on wire rack for 20 minutes and remove from pan.

Heath Bar Cake

I discovered Heath Bars during my senior year in college. (Frankly, my first Heath Bar was infinitely more exciting than my first fraternity party.) College was never the same after that initial died-and-gone-to-heaven taste sensation.

Consequently, I was elated, not long ago, when I discovered this recipe and I asked my sister to bake a Heath Bar Cake for me.

Before the cake had come out of the oven, my sister called with the bad news and the good news. "The ingredients cost $11.96!" she complained, justifiably indignant. But, Susan continued, the raw batter to this cake was the best she'd ever tasted in her life. She was even considering serving the batter in liquid form. ". . . in large wine glasses, I think, garnished with brown sugar," she mused.

"Call me when the cake is out of the oven," I said, quickly hanging up the phone.

Great batters usually make great cake, but I was a bit concerned when I didn't hear from my sister until the next day. As it happened, she'd gone to a neighbor's house for dinner and had taken along the Heath Bar Cake for dessert. "And was it a success?" I asked.

"More so than you can imagine!" Susan exclaimed. "The Laginestras devoured every last bite of it. And, you'll never believe this, but before we left, Michelle asked me for the recipe. I was astounded."

So was I. Michelle is six years old.

INGREDIENTS

2 cups flour, sifted
1 cup brown sugar

½ cup sugar
½ cup butter
1 cup chopped nuts
1 cup chocolate chips
7 Heath Bars, coarsely chopped
1 teaspoon baking soda
1 cup buttermilk
1 egg, beaten
1 teaspoon vanilla
¼ cup chopped nuts
2 Heath Bars, coarsely chopped

1. Preheat oven to 350°.
2. Mix flour and sugars in a large bowl.
3. Cut in butter until as fine as cornmeal. Set aside ½ cup of the mixture for topping.
4. Add the cup of nuts, chocolate chips, and 7 chopped Heath Bars to remaining flour mixture.
5. Add baking soda to buttermilk and stir into mixture.
6. Add egg and vanilla, stirring well.
7. Pour mixture into a prepared, greased and floured 9- × 13-inch pan.
8. Add ¼ cup nuts and 2 Heath Bars to reserved crumb mixture. Sprinkle over batter.
9. Bake in 350° oven for 35 minutes. Cool before serving.

By the way, I should point out that: 1) this recipe makes a very large cake (9- × 13-inch), and 2) it freezes very well. Cut the cake in two and freeze half for your next binge. It really is delicious. ("And worth $11.96," my sister adds.)

TIPS FOR HIDING FOOD:
Never hide Devil Dogs in your back pocket, especially if your jeans are as tight as mine.

Thomas Anderson's Favorite Chocolate-chocolate-chip Cake

ACTUALLY, I lied. I don't know if this is Thomas Anderson's favorite cake. As soon as he's old enough to talk (in about a year or two) I'll be sure to ask him.

What I do know is this is a favorite cake of Thomas's Mom because she was able to give me the ingredients and directions without consulting her recipe file.

1 box Duncan Hines Devil's Food Cake Mix
1 box instant chocolate pudding
4 eggs
¾ cup oil
½ cup warm water
8 ounces sour cream
12-ounce package of chocolate chips
Powdered confectioner's sugar

INGREDIENTS

1. Preheat oven to 350°.
2. Stir together the first 6 ingredients.
3. Add the chips at the last moment so they won't get too crushed.
4. Pour batter into a greased and floured bundt pan.
5. Bake in a 350° oven for about one hour or until a toothpick comes out clean.
6. Cool and sprinkle the top with confectioner's sugar.

Thomas's Mom warns not to use the powdered-sugar topping if you are making this as a birthday cake—unless, of course, you won't mind getting a faceful of sugar when the candles are blown out.

THERE are three very good reasons to travel:
1. See the world
2. Meet new people
3. Room service

Personally, I am more motivated by the third reason than any other. There is an art to room service and some hotels are more adept at it than others. For readers who are interested in room service, I am currently compiling a travel guide tentatively entitled: *Sign For Your Supper: A Guide to the Best Room Service in America*. Look for it in your bookstores and hotel lobbies.

Plain Jane's Travel Tips

Mimi's Triple Layer Chocolate Cake

MIMI is one of the *ladies* (as in . . . "Say hello to the ladies!") who plays canasta with my Mom. The ladies play at Mimi's house an awful lot. This is because of three reasons:

One, Mimi is a really good card player. Two, she's an incredible baker (and this chocolate cake proves it beyond a shadow of a doubt). And, last but most important, Mimi works in a cut-rate clothing store where she can get all the ladies (and the ladies' daughters) a discount on brand-name designer clothing (with the labels removed, of course).

What more could you ask of a friend besides canasta, chocolate cake, and Calvin Klein (wholesale, no less)?

INGREDIENTS

2¼ cups all purpose flour
1¾ cups sugar
1½ sticks butter, at room temperature
¾ cup milk
4 ounces (4 squares) unsweetened baking chocolate, melted
1½ teaspoons baking soda
1 teaspoon salt
¾ cup milk
3 eggs
1¼ teaspoons baking powder
1 teaspoon vanilla

Rich Chocolate Frosting
6 to 8 ounces unsweetened baking chocolate
¾ cup (1½ sticks) butter
4 cups sifted confectioner's sugar
6 tablespoons strongly brewed coffee
2 eggs
1 tablespoon vanilla
Pinch of salt
1 cup coarsely chopped toasted walnuts (optional)
1 cup toasted walnut halves

1. Preheat oven to 350° and grease three 9-inch layer-cake pans.
2. Sift flour into large bowl.
3. Add sugar, butter, ¾ cup milk, chocolate, baking soda, and salt. Beat 2 minutes with elec-

GO JAPANESE:
Making a Fashion Statement
with Hefty Bags

tric mixer at medium speed.

4. Add remaining milk, eggs, baking powder, and vanilla and beat for 2 more minutes.

5. Pour into prepared pans and bake in the middle of oven for 30 minutes or until cake tests done and has pulled away slightly from sides of pan. Allow to cool completely on racks.

6. Prepare frosting.

7. Soften chocolate and butter in top of double boiler over hot, not boiling, water and stir in remaining ingredients (but not the nuts).

8. Place top of double boiler in a bowl of ice and beat frosting with electric mixer about 5 minutes or until it reaches spreading consistency.

9. Place one cake layer on plate and frost. Sprinkle with ½ chopped nuts (if desired).

10. Place second layer on top and frost. Add remaining chopped nuts.

11. Frost top and sides of cake. Decorate with toasted walnut halves.

Plain Jane's Carrot Cake

IF your dinner menu calls for a vegetable—and you can't avoid the calling—then bake a carrot cake.

Although with the Galliano recipe, I have come out against scratch cakes, I must admit that there are some instances when a cake mix just can't compare with a truly great recipe. (That's why you'll find a few scratch cake recipes in my book.)

As far as I know, Betty Crocker has never perfected the carrot cake—so I did it for her. Here is a thick, moist cake invented solely for this cookbook.

Even though Plain Jane and carrots don't really fit together in one sentence, this is the instance where I could eat carrots all day.

INGREDIENTS

5 eggs
1½ cups sugar
2 cups all purpose flour
3 teaspoons baking powder
1 teaspoon salt
2 teaspoons baking soda

2 teaspoons cinnamon
1 cup vegetable oil
1 tablespoon vanilla
3 cups grated carrots
½ cup raisins
½ cup chopped walnuts
½ cup pineapple (drained and chopped)
½ cup coconut (optional)

Frosting:
8 ounces cream cheese
1 tablespoon butter
½ teaspoon vanilla
1 cup confectioner's sugar

1. Preheat oven to 325°.
2. In a large bowl, blend eggs and sugar.
3. In a separate bowl, sift all dry ingredients.
4. Alternate adding dry mixture and the oil to the sugar/egg mixture.
5. Add the vanilla.
6. Fold in the carrots, pineapple, nuts, raisins and coconut (if desired).
7. Lightly grease and dust a springform pan. Add batter and bake at 325° for one hour.
8. When completely cool, either powder lightly with confectioner's sugar or prepare frosting as follows: When all ingredients are at room temperature, blend them until smooth and spread on cake.

Dear Plain Jane,
  When I was a little girl. I could eat anything I wanted and I stayed skinny. I used to drink milk shakes for breakfast.
  Then, at 30, I had my first child and my metabolism went berserk. I don't seem to burn calories like I used to.
  What can I do?

  Desperate in Desoto

Dear Desperate,
  You'll have to do what the rest of us do—get fat.

  Jane

A basic rule of baking is that, in general, it's almost impossible to make an inedible batch of brownies.

Brownies are so elementary that you have to make a pretty serious mistake to totally ruin them. Simply overbaking, for example, will not do it. Many is the time I've cut away the burnt edges and eaten the center of a blackened pan of brownies. (I didn't eat the really black pieces until the next day.)

I suppose that if you forgot one of the main ingredients (say, the chocolate), you might be in some trouble. But, even then, a heavy topping of vanilla ice cream would probably salvage the remains.

I have no moral objection to boxed brownie mixes and think that Duncan Hines comes pretty close to making a great brownie (especially when served warm from the oven).

I did feel compelled, however, to include a scratch brownie recipe in this book as you can hardly discuss fattening foods without including brownies. So, I tested and retested various recipes and finally concluded that Laurie, my agent's associate, made the best brownies.

Laurie's secret ingredient is the chocolate chip. She says you can also use peanut butter chips but I prefer chocolate. Either way, remember you really can't go wrong—especially if you always stock an extra quart or two of vanilla ice cream in your freezer.

2 squares unsweetened baking chocolate
½ cup butter
2 large eggs
1 cup sugar
1 teaspoon vanilla
½ cup flour, unsifted
½ teaspoon baking powder
¼ teaspoon salt
½ cup chocolate chips or peanut butter chips
½ cup nuts (optional)

1. Preheat oven to 350° and grease an 8- × 8-inch pan.

The Bestest Brownies

A NEWLYWED CHECKLIST

☐ Salt
☐ Pepper
☐ Sugar
☐ Cinnamon
☐ Reddi-Wip
☐ Mayo
☐ Oreos
☐ Ketchup
☐ Soda
☐ Coffee
☐ Cigarettes
☐ Wine
☐ Champagne
☐ Scotch

INGREDIENTS

☐ Vodka
☐ Amaretto
☐ Bed

2. Melt chocolate and butter in a double boiler and set aside to cool.
3. Beat eggs and add sugar.
4. Add vanilla and chocolate-butter mixture.
5. Add flour, baking powder, and salt.
6. Fold in chips (and nuts, if desired).
7. Pour into pan and bake for 30 to 40 minutes or until done.

Caution: Do not attempt to taste the chocolate batter before you've added the sugar. When taste-testing the raw batter, be sure to include one chocolate chip with each taste.

Dear Plain Jane,
    What is an appropriate menu for a casual Tupperware party?

Jackie O.
Manhattan, N.Y.

Dear Jackie,
    Whenever you throw a party, it's nice to coordinate your food with the theme of the gathering.
    In the case of a Tupperware party, you could serve foods that have been processed from the same petroleum base as the plastic service ware.
    I'd recommend aerosol cheeses served on processed potato chips and a sweet side-dish made with anything labeled "Artificially Sweetened Dessert Topping."
    Use your own imagination or call your local Texaco station for other party hints.

Jane

Sandra's Mother's Frozen Chocolate Velvet Pie

SANDRA'S mother makes the best chocolate pie I've ever tasted—bar none and no exaggeration. That's why I've sacrificed a lot to get this recipe for my readers—making several long distance calls to Washington and Massachusetts and gaining 4½ pounds testing it in my own kitchen. If you don't appreciate the effort, then it's your loss and, as I said, my gain.
    Aside from the taste and texture (they don't call

it *velvet* for nothing), the beauty of this pie is that it'll keep in your freezer for up to three months, unless of course, you allow anyone in your family to taste it first.

Crust:
3 egg whites
¼ teaspoon salt
6 tablespoons sugar
3 cups finely chopped walnuts

Filling:
6 tablespoons light corn syrup
4 teaspoons water
2 tablespoons vanilla
12-ounce bag semisweet chocolate bits
1 can condensed (not evaporated) milk, chilled for at least 24 hours
2 cups heavy whipping cream

1. Preheat oven to 400°.
2. For crust, beat whites and salt till soft peaks form and then gradually beat in sugar until stiff peaks form.
3. Add nuts. Spread mixture over the bottom and up the sides of a greased 10-inch pie plate. Continue the mixture slightly over the edge of the plate.
4. Bake 10 to 12 minutes. Cool thoroughly.
5. For filling, stir corn syrup and water in a pan until it *just* boils and then remove from heat.
6. Quickly stir in vanilla and chocolate bits until chocolate is completely melted. Cool. Set aside two tablespoons of this chocolate mixture.
7. Pour the rest of the mixture into a large mixing bowl and add the milk and cream. Blend at low speed and then beat at medium speed until soft peaks form.
8. Pour filling into pie shell and freeze, uncovered, until firm.
9. When firm, pipe on reserved chocolate with writing tube or drizzle on with a spoon (*or* use chocolate curls instead).
10. Store wrapped in freezer for up to three months.

INGREDIENTS

THE WORLD OF WOKS—
Stir-frying is only one of the many ways to use your wok. Did you know, for instance, that the wok makes a perfect sundae dish?

To season for dessert use, fill with two quarts of Jamoca Almond Fudge ice cream and lick clean.

Chocolate Mousse Pie

I asked Sandra's mother for her recipe for Frozen Chocolate Velvet Pie and, as a bonus, she also sent me the recipe for this heavenly concoction.

You might think that this pie is fattening because of the high-calorie ingredients—heavy cream, chocolate wafers, sugar, and such. But think of it this way: Chocolate Mousse Pie is so rich, you can't possibly eat more than a single slice (well, maybe just a *sliver* for seconds). It's got to be less fattening than a pint of Haagen-Dazs, right?

INGREDIENTS

Crust:
3 cups chocolate wafer crumbs
½ cup (1 stick) unsalted butter, melted

Filling:
1 pound semisweet chocolate
2 eggs
4 egg yolks
2 cups whipping cream
6 tablespoons confectioner's sugar
4 egg whites, at room temperature

Topping:
2 cups whipping cream
Sugar

Tips for RANSACKING THE COOKIE JAR:
Only eat the broken cookies—you can keep eating pieces and never feel like you've eaten a whole cookie.

1. For crust, combine crumbs and butter.
2. Press mixture on bottom and up the sides of a 10-inch springform pan and refrigerate for 30 minutes (or chill in the freezer).
3. For filling, in a double boiler (over simmering water) melt chocolate and let cool to lukewarm (95° on a candy thermometer).
4. Add whole eggs and mix well. Add yolks and mix thoroughly.
5. Whip cream with confectioner's sugar until soft peaks form. Set aside.
6. In another bowl, beat egg whites until stiff but not dry.
7. Lighten the chocolate by first stirring in a little bit of the cream mixture and then some of the whites mixture.

8. Fold in remaining cream and whites until completely incorporated.
9. Turn into crust and chill at least six hours or, preferably, overnight.
10. Whip remaining 2 cups cream (with sugar to taste) until quite stiff.
11. Loosen crust on all sides using a sharp knife and remove springform. Spread all but ½ cup cream over top. Pipe remaining cream into rosettes in center of pie. Garnish with chocolate curls.

The mousse filling can be prepared ahead and frozen. Thaw overnight in fridge.

I leave out the rosettes part in Step #11 because I'd rather eat whipped cream than sculpt it.

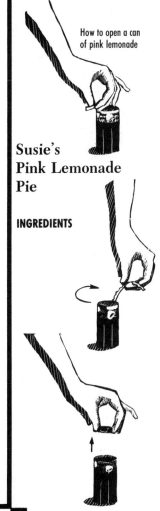

How to open a can
of pink lemonade

THIS recipe requires two basic cooking techniques: opening a can and pouring. If you can perform those two functions, you can easily make this pie.

Susie's Pink Lemonade Pie

INGREDIENTS

1 14-ounce can sweetened condensed milk
1 6-ounce can frozen pink lemonade, thawed
Juice of 1 lemon
1 package of frozen raspberries or strawberries, thawed
1 9-inch graham cracker crust, baked and cooled
Heavy cream (whipped)

1. Stir together milk, lemonade, and lemon juice.
2. Pour into baked crust.
3. Refrigerate for 24 hours. (Do not freeze!)
4. Top with whipped cream before serving.
5. When serving, pour a tablespoon (or three or five) of the thawed raspberries (or strawberries) over each individual piece of pie.

Susie said to tell you that this is a very refreshing pie—perfect for after a heavy meal.

Hershey Bar Pie

Crust (will make two crusts):
½ cup butter
1 cup sugar
1 egg
1 teaspoon vanilla
1¼ cups unsifted all purpose flour
½ cup Hershey's Cocoa
¾ teaspoon baking soda
¼ teaspoon salt

Filling:
1 Giant Hershey Milk Chocolate Bar (8 ounces)
⅓ cup milk
1½ cups miniature marshmallows
1 cup heavy cream
Whipped topping
1 can cherry pie filling (optional)

1. Preheat oven to 375°.
2. Prepare crust by creaming butter, sugar, egg, and vanilla.
3. Combine flour, cocoa, baking soda, and salt and add to creamed mixture.
4. Shape soft dough into two 1½-inch-thick rolls. Wrap in waxed paper and plastic wrap and chill until firm.
5. Cut one roll into ⅛-inch slices and arrange, edges touching, on bottom and up sides of a greased 9-inch pie pan (small spaces in crust will not affect pie).
6. Bake at 375° for 8 to 10 minutes. Cool.
7. For filling, break chocolate bar into pieces and melt with milk in the top of a double boiler over hot water.
8. Add marshmallows, stirring until melted, and cool completely.
9. Whip cream until stiff and fold into chocolate mixture.
10. Spoon into crust. Cover and chill until firm.
11. Garnish with whipped topping or chilled cherry pie filling.

I asked Emily to send me a recipe for my book and this is what I received—Brandy Alexander Pie. Now, I'm not complaining, this is a dynamite pie. However, I had asked for an *entree* recipe and this is what I got.

Well, Emily and I obviously think alike—Brandy Alexander Pie does make the perfect main course for any Plain Jane dinner.

Crust:
1½ cups graham cracker crumbs
⅓ cup melted butter

Filling:
½ cup cold water
1 enveloped unflavored gelatin
3 eggs, separated
⅔ cup sugar
⅛ teaspoon salt
¼ cup crème de cacao
¼ cup cognac
1 cup heavy cream

1. Preheat oven to 350°.
2. Prepare crust by mixing graham cracker crumbs and butter. Press into pie plate and bake at 350° for 10 minutes (or buy and bake a prepared crust). Allow crust to cool.
3. Pour water into a saucepan and sprinkle in the gelatin.
4. Stir in the three egg yolks, ⅓ cup of the sugar, and salt.
5. Place over low heat and stir until gelatin is dissolved and the mixture starts to thicken. *Don't let it boil*. Remove from heat.
6. Stir in the crème de cacao and cognac. Chill just until mixture starts to mound slightly. Watch it—it can turn to lumpy Jello if you let it cool too much. Then your pie will have little rubbery lumps through it, which is gross (Emily's description).
7. Beat egg whites until stiff. Add the remaining sugar and beat until peaks form.
8. Fold this meringue into the thickened yolk mixture.

Emily's Brandy Alexander Pie

INGREDIENTS

9. Whip the cream and fold into the mixture, too.
10. Turn mixture into the crust. You can garnish with a little unsweetened, finely grated chocolate—just a dusting in the middle or a ring around the edges for decoration.
11. Chill for several hours or overnight.

Dear Plain Jane,
    How can I prevent butter from scorching?
                                    Debbie B.
                                    Hollywood, Ca.

Dear Debbie,
    Don't iron it so often.

                                    Jane

Rich Rhubarb Cream Pie

MY sister and I had just returned from four blissful days at the seashore doing what we most enjoy: eating, napping, and eating again. I felt completely rested and 10 pounds overweight.

Impulsively, I decided to diet until my next vacation (the following weekend) and I was halfway through a medium-sized container of cottage cheese when my doorbell rang. In walked Deran, my upstairs neighbor, carrying a plateful of Rich Rhubarb Cream Pie. "Here's a sample of my friend Dick Kimball's best pie—and the recipe for your book," Deran said.

Now, many of my friends provided recipes for this book, but Deran was the only one smart enough to also bring along a big sample for me to eat. Pushing aside the cottage cheese, I proceeded to devour this luscious pie and it was just about the best lunch I'd had all week. (And considering the food I'd eaten at the shore, that is really saying something.)

So, the next time you feel compelled to eat cottage cheese for lunch, follow the Plain Jane example and whip up this pie instead. I guarantee you it'll taste better.

Crust:
1¼ cups flour
6 tablespoons sweet butter
Pinch of salt
3 to 4 tablespoons cold water

Filling:
1 pint heavy cream
4 egg yolks
1¼ cups sugar
¼ teaspoon salt
2 tablespoons flour
2 cups raw rhubarb, diced

Meringue topping:
4 egg whites
½ teaspoon cream of tartar
4 teaspoons powdered sugar
½ teaspoon orange extract

INGREDIENTS

1. Use your favorite pastry crust or combine all of the crust ingredients listed and chill for at least one hour.
2. Preheat oven to 400°.
3. Roll out crust and fit into a 9- or 10-inch pie plate, making a high, crimped edge. Chill while preparing filling.
4. For filling, beat cream and egg yolks together.
5. Combine sugar, salt, and flour and stir into cream mixture.
6. Spread rhubarb in pie shell and slowly pour cream mixture over it.
7. Bake for 15 minutes in preheated 400° oven and then reduce temperature to 350°. Bake until center of pie is thick when cut with a knife, about 40 minutes. Cool slightly.
8. For meringue, beat egg whites until stiff and firm peaks form. (Beat in cream of tartar.)
9. Continue beating while adding powdered sugar until thick and creamy; flavor with orange extract.
10. Cover pie with meringue and bake approximately 15 minutes in a 350° oven or until golden brown. Cool before serving.

Susan's Roommate-From-College's Frozen Yogurt Pie

THIS may surprise my readers, but I am a great fan of yogurt. It is a natural, low-fat food that is popular among fashion models, fast-track executives, and me.

The only difference between them and me is that I never lose any weight eating yogurt. I don't understand why. Everyone says that yogurt is dietetic. Yet I eat it all the time and it never makes me any thinner. Of course, I prefer frozen yogurt over the kind that is sold in a container. I know frozen yogurt has a little more sugar in it, but then, I never seem to get enough sugar in my diet.

Anyway, dietetic or not, you've really got to admire frozen yogurt—it tries so hard to taste like ice cream. It even tries to look like soft ice cream—processed in those same metal air machines. I feel sort of obligated to buy a frozen yogurt every time I pass a yogurt store. I always remind myself that I'm eating something not quite as fattening as Carvel, and it makes me feel very self-sacrificing.

But, enough about store-bought frozen yogurt. In your own home, without an air machine, you can make a really good frozen yogurt pie. With very little effort, you, too, can duplicate that "almost ice cream" taste.

This recipe comes from my hippie days in college. (Yes, Plain Jane was once a hippie—I had hair to my waist, ate sprouts, listened to *Big Pink*, and watched Woodstock on television.) Frozen yogurt wasn't available back then. In the grocery store, we could only buy Dannon—designer yogurt hadn't been invented yet. (Life was simpler in the 60s.) We made Frozen Yogurt Pie in college when our entire kitchen consisted of a miniature refrigerator hidden in the dorm closet.

I suppose you could make this recipe with a classier yogurt than Dannon, but, somehow, it just wouldn't be the same.

Do make sure you use genuine ingredients in this pie: real Cool Whip and a prepared graham cracker crust. If you fancy it up too much, no one will recognize it—not even Susan's roommate from college, who gave me the recipe in the first place.

INGREDIENTS

2 8-ounce containers of your favorite flavor yogurt (use two different flavors for variety)
1 large container of Cool Whip (no substitutes!)
About 1 cup (or more) of fruit (use whatever you have in the house—strawberries, blueberries, pineapple, etc.). Use canned fruit if you don't have fresh.
1 prepared graham cracker crust

1. Mix together all the ingredients.
2. Pour into the graham cracker crust.
3. Freeze (about 3 hours).

You can sprinkle the top with raisins, chocolate chips, coconut, crushed Oreo cookies, M&Ms, etc. Add an extra dollop of Cool Whip if you really like the stuff. Serve cold, with Bob Dylan music playing in the background.

Dear Plain Jane,
    Why does fattening food taste so much better than dietetic food?
    Wouldn't it make more sense if it was the other way around?

Clara B.
Santa Monica, Ca.

Dear Clara,
    What kind of dumb question is that?
    Fattening food tastes better because of two things—sugar and sour cream.
    If the Lord had meant it the other way around, would He have invented Weight Watchers?

Jane

    P.S. If you are going to spend 20¢ to write me, then you'd better start coming up with smarter questions.

M&M Cookies

Shown actual size

ALONG with the truly great inventions of this century, such as the Salk vaccine, the assembly line, and the microchip, I think it only fitting to include the M&M.

I suppose all major inventions started with a simple idea, but consider, for a moment, the creative impulse that inspired the M&M. Imagine, one day a guy sat down and said to himself, "Today I will invent a chocolate pill." And then, luckily for us, he did.

The world has not forgotten this awesome deed. The M&M has been immortalized for all time by my friend Laurie (yes, she's also the genius behind the brownie recipe). Here she uses M&Ms in place of chocolate chips for cookies that, truly, merit the Nobel Prize.

INGREDIENTS

1 stick sweet butter
¼ cup light brown sugar
½ cup sugar
1 egg
½ teaspoon vanilla
1 cup plus 2 tablespoons flour
½ teaspoon salt
½ teaspoon baking soda
6 ounces or so of M&Ms

1. Preheat oven to 350°.
2. Cream butter and add sugars.
3. Add egg and vanilla.
4. Sift together the flour, salt, and baking soda and add to butter-sugar mixture.
5. Mix in M&Ms, being careful not to crush them while mixing.
6. Using a teaspoon, drop cookies onto a greased cookie sheet.
7. Dot each cookie with one or two extra M&Ms.
8. Bake in 350° oven for 8 to 10 minutes or until browned.

Grocery tip: When buying the ingredients for these cookies, I purchase the One Pounder bag of M&Ms. I use 6 ounces for the recipe, and the rest are for me.

Chocolate Chip/ Potato Chip Cookies

ACTUALLY, I shouldn't be giving you this recipe because I haven't yet gotten permission to reprint it.

I found this recipe in a book called *The 47 Best Chocolate Chip Cookies in the World*. I tested many of these 47 recipes before I decided on this one, invented by Lucille Boyce in Burbank, California. Here, Lucille combines chocolate chips with potato chips to make a really great cookie. (Don't snicker until you've actually tasted one of these beauties.)

INGREDIENTS

1 cup plus 2 tablespoons all purpose flour
½ teaspoon baking soda
¼ teaspoon salt
½ cup butter or shortening
¾ cup light brown sugar, firmly packed
1 teaspoon vanilla
1 egg, well beaten
¾ cup (6 ounces) chocolate chips
¾ cup potato chips, crushed

1. Preheat oven to 375°.
2. Sift together flour, soda, salt and set aside.
3. Beat together butter and brown sugar until fluffy.
4. Add vanilla and egg, beating well.
5. Gradually add dry ingredients and mix thoroughly.
6. Stir in chocolate chips and potato chips.
7. Drop by teaspoonfuls onto ungreased cookie sheet, about 2 inches apart.
8. Bake for 10 to 12 minutes or until lightly browned. Cool on racks.

About that wee problem with the permission to reprint this recipe: I just noticed the publisher of *47 Best Recipes* is St. Martin's, the publisher of *Plain Jane's Thrill of Very Fattening Foods Cookbook*. What a coincidence!

Doug's Cookies

HONESTLY, I don't know anyone named Doug so you may be curious as to why these cookies bear his name. Frankly, I haven't a clue.

My friend Diane sent this recipe with no explanation of the name. And now she's off to Florida for a vacation so I can't ask her.

Well, don't worry, Diane. I won't mention a word of this to your husband, Sol.

INGREDIENTS

1 cup margarine or butter
5 tablespoons sugar
1 teaspoon vanilla
2 cups flour

Frosting:
1 cup sifted confectioner's sugar
2 tablespoons cocoa
2 tablespoons hot water
½ teaspoon vanilla

How to shape Crescents

1. Preheat oven to 400°.
2. Cream margarine and add sugar, vanilla, and flour.
3. Roll level tablespoons of mixture into balls.
4. Place on greased cookie sheet and flatten slightly.
5. Bake at 400° for 10 to 12 minutes.
6. Combine frosting ingredients and dot each baked cookie.

Almond Crescents

½ pound butter
¾ cup sugar
2 cups flour
2 egg yolks
¼ pound sliced almonds, crushed
Powdered sugar

1. Preheat oven to 350°.
2. Add sugar to softened butter.
3. Slowly add flour, one yolk at a time, and crushed almonds. Mix well with hands.
4. Make crescents by elongating a teaspoonful ball of dough, turning in the edges and shaping

into crescent.

5. Bake at 350° for 10 to 12 minutes. Dip hot cookies in powdered sugar.

Grandmother Avignone's Zabaglione

I don't have an Italian grandmother so I had to borrow one from Carol Reo Floriani. (With a name like Reo Floriani, Carol had to have at least one great Italian recipe in her family. And she did!)

Zabaglione is a wine-custard dessert from Northern Italy. I've eaten it lots of times on expense-account lunches in fancy Italian restaurants where it's the priciest dessert on the menu. (It's usually prepared at your table by the same waiter who tosses the Caesar salad.)

Zabaglione turnes out to be a really simple dessert that you can easily (and inexpensively) prepare in your own kitchen. You don't have to be Italian to make this dessert, but it helps to practice a few times before making it for a crowd.

INGREDIENTS

8 egg yolks
5 tablespoons sugar
¾ cup Harvey's Bristol Cream, comparable sherry, or Marsala wine
1 cup heavy sweet cream

1. Separate eggs, making sure not to get any egg white into the yolks. (Even a slight amount of egg white will make the mixture grainy when it's cooked.)
2. Whisk the egg yolks with the sugar in the top of a double boiler. Place over simmering water.
3. Slowly add the sherry, whisking constantly. Remove from the heat as soon as the sauce becomes thick and foamy. Chill.
4. Whip one cup of heavy cream and fold into the cooled mixture. Spoon into dessert dishes.

Makes 6 (normal), 4 (large), 2 (humongous) or 1 (Plain Jane) serving, depending on your appetite and/or heritage. (Now that's Italian!)

FIVE METHODS FOR BUYING CHOCOLATE CHIP COOKIES

1) Taste one before buying.

2) Bite one before buying.

3) Sample one before buying.

4) Try one before buying.

5) Eat one before buying.

Jello Trifle Supreme

WARNING: This dessert will take at least 24 hours to assemble. It's a ton of work so don't even attempt it unless you are extremely patient and more than slightly compulsive.

If you're still with me, then read on.

Jello Trifle Supreme is meant to be adapted to your own particular palate. I will give you the general idea of how to assemble the layers and my suggestions for various possibilities but use your own imagination and select the ingredients your family enjoys. If, for instance, you love coconut but hate marshmallow, then adjust this recipe accordingly. Remember that it is almost impossible to make a wrong combination in this dessert. (Unless you're one of those fanatics who shops in health food stores and adds wheat germ to every recipe.)

To assemble this dessert, you'll need a very large glass bowl shaped like a brandy glass. (Or you can use a punch bowl, but do make this dessert in a glass container because it is quite colorful when finished.)

Make this dessert for a crowd—it's simply too much work (and too much dessert) for a small group. The last time I made Jello Trifle Supreme was for my nephew Adam's third birthday party. Everyone at the party, adults and kids alike, loved it—everyone except Adam, that is. He was upset about not getting a traditional birthday cake with candles. Luckily, my sister, my mother, and I had also prepared four ice box cakes (see recipe on pg. 15). We made four cakes because each one was molded into a letter that, together, spelled ADAM. Yes, compulsive behavior runs rampant in my family.

INGREDIENTS

*5 or 6 boxes of Jello in different flavors and
   colors—cherry, orange, lemon, lime, grape.
3 boxes instant pudding—chocolate, vanilla,
   strawberry
Chocolate chips
Coconut
Raisins
Mandarin oranges
Chopped walnuts*

42

Maraschino cherries
Miniature marshmallows
Canned peaches
Peanut brittle, crushed
Sprinkles
Heavy cream (whipped)

1. Make one box of Jello (with ice cubes, as indicated on package, to speed up setting.) Pour into brandy glass serving bowl.
2. Add coconut to Jello.
3. Place in refrigerator and chill until set.
4. When Jello is firmly set, prepare one box of pudding and let it cool for a few minutes in the refrigerator before spooning on top of Jello layer. (Hot pudding will melt the Jello.) Sprinkle with crushed peanut brittle and return to refrigerator.
5. Be careful not to smear the sides of the glass with any excess pudding as you build up each layer.
6. Prepare another box of Jello and pour over set pudding layer. Add mandarin oranges.
7. Keep alternating layers of pudding, candy, Jello, and fruit. Remember to allow sufficient time between layers for pudding and Jello to set. (This is why the Trifle takes up to 24 hours to prepare.)
8. Continue layering until a few inches from the top of the bowl. Before serving, cover the top layer with whipped cream. Add sprinkles and cherries for color.

When serving, be sure to scoop parts from several different layers with each portion. Each spoonful of this dessert provides a different taste sensation.

Dear Plain Jane,
    Do you recommend using a microwave oven?
                                            Cheryl K.
                                    Woodcliff Lake, N.J.
Dear Cheryl,
    Only if you enjoy x-ray treatments and radiation leakage.
                                                    Jane

Lynn's Amaretto Mold

AMARETTO is my favorite after-dinner liquor. (I also like it before dinner, after lunch, during lunch, and after breakfast.) So, I was really interested in getting this recipe from Lynn.

Lynn says she actually makes this recipe with Cool Whip but that I should list whipped cream because it's more fattening. I'm not sure that whipped toppings are exactly dietetic; but, for those of you on a restricted diet, follow Lynn's advice and save calories with Cool Whip.

INGREDIENTS

3 envelopes unflavored gelatin
⅓ cup sugar
1 cup Amaretto
2 cups (1 pint) half-and-half
1 can (1 pound, 14 ounces) apricot halves,
   drained and dried
2 cups heavy cream, whipped (or Cool Whip)
Additional whipped cream and apricot halves

1. In saucepan, combine gelatin, sugar, and Amaretto.
2. Stir over low heat until gelatin dissolves.
3. Stir in half-and-half.
4. Chill until mixture thickens slightly.
5. Fold in apricots and whipped cream (or Cool Whip).
6. Pour into soufflé dish. (Lynn uses a Tupperware mold.)
7. Chill until firm.
8. When ready to serve, top with apricot quarters and whipped cream for decoration.

BASIC KITCHEN EQUIPMENT

Pot

Spatula

Ginsu knife

Telephone

Measuring spoon

Tupperware—97 piece starter set

Dear Plain Jane,
    I work all day and then come home to my three kids. I'm just too tired to cook.
    Sometimes, I bring home a take-out pizza or fried chicken but my husband always complains that the kids aren't getting enough vegetables that way.
    What can a mother do?

Curious in Kansas

Dear Curious,
    Take out pizza with green peppers and onions.

Jane

Ann's Amaretti Cream Topping

WHIP a pint of heavy cream with 1 tablespoon confectioner's sugar. Add 2 tablespoons of sherry or Amaretto liquor and 3 cups of crushed Amaretti cookies. Serve over rich pound cake and sprinkle with brown sugar.
    Note: Ann says all ingredients can be adjusted to taste. Add more liquor if you feel adventurous.

Pudding by Mr. Tux

1 box chocolate pudding
8 Amaretti cookies, crumbled
Lemon peels
Whipped heavy cream

1. Cook the pudding as directed on package.
2. Add 6 crumbled cookies and lemon peels to mixture.
3. Chill in mold. Remove when firm and top with whipped cream and more crushed cookies.

Note: Amaretti cookies are an incredible taste sensation and, crumbled, the perfect topping for almost any sweet dessert. If you can't get them in your area, order by mail from Williams-Sonoma, P.O. Box 7456, San Francisco, California 94120-7456 *or* Manganaro Foods, 488 Ninth Avenue, New York, New York 10018.

Susan's Toblerone Mousse

INGREDIENTS

YOU have to love Toblerone to love this recipe but that's not exactly hard to do. If you don't love Toblerone chocolate, you've never tasted Toblerone chocolate.

7 ounces Toblerone milk chocolate
6 tablespoons boiling water
½ cup heavy cream
2 egg whites
pinch of salt
2 tablespoons sugar

1. Melt chocolate with water in small but heavy saucepan over a low heat. Stir occasionally with a wire whisk till chocolate is melted and smooth. Do not overheat.
2. When chocolate is smooth, remove from heat and set aside till cool.
3. Whip cream in small bowl until it holds a soft shape. Set aside.
4. Beat egg whites and salt in small bowl until it holds a soft shape.
5. Add sugar to egg whites gradually and continue to beat until mixture holds a firm shape.
6. Chill chocolate briefly in freezer, stirring occasionally, till it thickens (but don't let it start to harden).
7. Fold chocolate, whites, and cream until incorporated.
8. Pour into serving bowl or wine glasses.
9. Cover and refrigerate.
10. About 1½ hours before serving, place in freezer. (It should have the consistency of creamy ice cream when ready to serve.)

A large serving bowl will need more time in the freezer. If you are serving directly after preparing, put the mousse right into the freezer. Serves 4.

TO the best of my knowledge, my mother's friend Flo never claimed to be a great cook. Not that it ever seemed to bother her too much. "Crazy Flo," as she is affectionately nicknamed, is better known for her flamboyant sense of humor and her ability to conduct endless conversations with complete strangers.

I knew that Flo wanted to contribute to my book when she started telling me about her mousse recipe.

"Great," I said, "Mail me the recipe." A week later I received the following:

2 Cool Whips (1 large, 1 medium size)
2 tablespoons instant coffee (mixed with water)
¼ cup cocoa
¼ cup Kahlua
2 tablespoons sugar
Grated chocolate for topping

The problem here is that I'm not quite sure what you're supposed to do with all these ingredients. Flo didn't include any directions with her list of ingredients.

All she wrote was that this ". . . can be frozen or refrigerated as desired."

I'd give you Flo's telephone number so that you could call her to get the instructions, but I warn you—no phone call to Flo lasts less than 45 minutes so be prepared to reveal the innermost details of your personal life before you find out when to add the cocoa.

Flo's Cool-Whip Mousse

INGREDIENTS

Dear Plain Jane,
   Why does a lobster turn red when put in boiling water?
                                   Curious in Conn.

Dear Curious,
   He's madder than hell.
   Wouldn't you be?

                                   Jane

White-Chocolate Mousse with Strawberry Sauce in Tuile Shells

THIS dessert gets the prize as the recipe with the longest title and the most ingredients.

Don't think of this as "cooking"—here, you are creating a masterpiece.

You'll have to bake the Tuiles (cookies), puree the strawberries, and then prepare the mousse, but, in the end, you'll have one fabulous dessert.

Anyway, if you think *this* is a lot of work, turn to Jello Trifle Supreme (pg. 42) and this will look like a snap.

INGREDIENTS

Cookies:
6 *tablespoons (¾ pound) butter, at room temperature*
½ *cup sugar*
1 *cup sliced almonds*
2 *egg whites*
⅓ *cup sifted all purpose flour*
Pinch of salt

Mousse:
¼ *pound sugar cubes*
¼ *cup water*
½ *cup egg whites (from about 4 large eggs), at room temperature*
1 *pound imported white chocolate, cut into very small cubes (the better the chocolate, the better the mousse)*
2 *cups whipping cream, well chilled*

Sauce:
2 *pints strawberries, washed and hulled*
2 *tablespoons kirsch*
1 *tablespoon sugar*
Pinch of salt
Fresh mint leaves for garnish

1. To make *cookie shells*, preheat oven to 400° and butter a heavy-duty baking sheet.
2. Cream butter and sugar thoroughly.
3. Stir in almonds, egg whites, flour, and salt.
4. Drop batter onto sheet by tablespoons, leaving enough space for spreading.
5. Bake about 10 minutes or until cookies are golden brown around edges and slightly yellow

FOOD STORAGE:
Pepperidge Farm cookies keep better when stored under your bed, in the drawer of your night table, or under your pillow.

in center.

6. Remove from sheet with spatula and immediately press onto rolling pin to give cookies a curved shape. Let stand several minutes.

7. Remove and cool on rack. (About 1 dozen large cookies.)

How to shape Tuile Shells

8. To make *mousse*, combine sugar cubes and water in saucepan and bring to boil, stirring or shaking pot occasionally until sugar melts.

9. Cook without stirring until syrup reaches hardball stage (when dropped in very cold water, syrup will form a hard ball—about 255° on a candy thermometer).

10. Whip egg whites to form soft peaks; then reduce speed of beater and slowly add sugar syrup.

11. Beat in chocolate pieces (they will melt partially) and cool to lukewarm.

12. Whip cream until stiff and fold into chocolate mixture. Chill at least 4 hours.

13. To make *sauce*, puree strawberries and stir in remaining sauce ingredients, except mint.

14. Cover and chill thoroughly.

15. To serve, place strawberry sauce on tuile shell and top with mousse. Garnish with a fresh mint leaf and a little more sauce.

There, now, that wasn't so hard, was it?

Fattening Fruit Salad

FRUIT salad can be greatly enhanced by the addition of a few extra ingredients such as liquor, sherbet, ice cream, and cake.

To start, select your favorite fruits—peaches, melons, pineapples, whatever is in season. Just be sure to include large quantities of the more fattening fruits like grapes, cherries, and bananas.

Next, add a cup or two of fresh orange juice or canned apricot juice (or some of both).

Then add a generous dose of Cassis. Cassis is a blackcurrant liquor and it has a lovely deep raspberry hue to it. Cassis will heighten both the color and the alcoholic content of your fruit salad.

Finally, be sure to add the ingredients that really bring out the flavor of the fruit—raspberry sherbet and vanilla ice cream piled high over a nice solid base like Galliano Cake (see recipe on pg. 19) or a defrosted Sara Lee Pound Cake.

Even though this dessert is loaded with calories, you can get up from the table telling yourself you had only a fruit salad for dessert.

PLAIN JANE'S 15 FAVORITE FRESH FRUIT DISHES

Peach Melba	Cherry Coke	Plum Pudding
Banana Split	Apricot Preserves	Pineapple Upside-Down Cake
Blueberry Pancakes	Fig Newtons	Coconut Custard
Strawberry Shortcake	Key Lime Pie	Raisinets
Apple Crisp	Lemon Jello	Grape Kool-Aid

My Sister's Apple Crisp

IN the early fall, my sister and I like to go apple picking in upstate New York. You are allowed to roam among the apple orchards and pick fruit till you can hardly lift your basket. We love getting out in the country air, picking the fruit, and then racing home to bake this fattening Apple Crisp. Isn't nature grand?

6 tart apples (I prefer green apples)
2 cups sugar
¼ teaspoon ground cloves
½ teaspoon cinnamon
2 teaspoons lemon juice
¾ cup sifted flour
⅛ teaspoon salt
6 tablespoons butter
¼ cup chopped nuts

1. Preheat oven to 350°.
2. Peel, core, and slice apples.
3. Add 1½ cups sugar, spices, and lemon juice. Mix lightly.
4. Pour into a deep, buttered casserole.
5. Blend remaining sugar, flour, salt, and butter to crumbly texture.
6. Add nuts and sprinkle over apple mixture.
7. Bake for 45 minutes or until apples are tender.

It goes without saying that, like all great apple recipes, this dessert is greatly enhanced when topped with a huge amount of your favorite flavor ice cream.

Adam's Apples and Peanut Butter

MY nephew, Adam, only eats apples when they are coated with a thick layer of peanut butter. (He says you can use either chunky or regular.) He also likes peanut butter with honey on bread.

Chocolate Peanut Butter Cheesecake

SOMETIMES the shortest introductions are also the best and, sometimes, a few words can speak volumes. I think that a basic description of this dessert is all that is needed: Here's a cheesecake made with ice cream and peanut butter. That should be enough to send any true Plain Jane racing to the grocery store for ingredients.

INGREDIENTS

1 8½-ounce package chocolate wafers, crushed into crumbs
⅓ cup melted butter
1 quart plus 1 pint Baskin-Robbins Chocolate Fudge ice cream
2 egg whites
¼ cup sugar
1 cup whipping cream
1 8-ounce package cream cheese
¾ cup sugar
1 teaspoon vanilla
¾ cup creamy peanut butter
2 egg yolks

THE THREE
MOST ADMIRED WOMEN
IN AMERICA:

Nancy Reagan

Betty Crocker

Aunt Jemima

1. Combine chocolate crumbs and butter. Mix well.
2. Press all but 1 cup of mixture on bottom and about ¾ inch up the sides of a 10-inch springform pan. (Reserve remaining crumbs for topping.)
3. Using quart of ice cream, spade thin sheets of ice cream around sides of pan. Smooth ice cream into ½″ thick, even layer. (If ice cream becomes too soft, return to freezer for about 20 minutes until firm.) Be careful not to disturb crumb crust. Place in freezer while preparing peanut butter filling.
4. Beat egg whites until soft peaks form.
5. Gradually add ¼ cup sugar and beat until mixture forms stiff peaks.
6. Whip cream and place in refrigerator.
7. Combine cream cheese, ¾ cup sugar, vanilla, and peanut butter in mixing bowl. Blend thoroughly.
8. Add egg yolks, one at a time, beating until well blended.
9. Gently fold in whipped cream, then egg whites.
10. Remove springform pan from freezer, add

peanut butter filling and freeze.
11. When set, cover top of dessert with a layer of ice cream, using remaining pint.
12. Sprinkle reserved cookie crumbs over ice cream. Freeze for at least 1 hour.
13. Allow to soften slightly in the refrigerator for 10-15 minutes before cutting. Makes 12 servings.

JUNIOR'S Restaurant/Bakery specializes in cheesecake and they have to make a great cheesecake because they cater to the Brooklyn/Miami Beach crowd.

What's amazing about their recipe, however, is that it's so simple to make.

Junior's Famous Cheesecake

INGREDIENTS

⅞ cup sugar
2 tablespoons cornstarch
1 pound 14 ounces cream cheese
1 extra large egg
½ cup heavy cream
¾ teaspoon vanilla
Graham crackers, crushed (enough for a 7-inch pan)
Butter

1. Preheat oven to 450°.
2. Mix sugar with cornstarch.
3. Add to cream cheese and mix.
4. Add egg and blend.
5. Add heavy cream, a little bit at a time, and mix.
6. Add vanilla and mix.
7. Prepare pan by greasing it well and patting down a layer of graham cracker crumbs. Cover with cheese mixture.
8. Bake at 450° for about 40 to 50 minutes or until top is golden brown.
9. Cool for about 3 hours.

Cooking with Ice Cream

Seven Utensils for Eating Ice Cream:

Teaspoon

Soup spoon

Tablespoon

Ice cream scooper

Ladle

Measuring cup

Snow shovel

Peanut Brittle Fudge Squares

IF I had to pick my favorite weakness, it would be ice cream. I can do without a lot of material things in life but ice cream is definitely not one of them.

Eating ice cream is as natural to me as breathing and, like breathing, I wouldn't—couldn't—think of giving it up.

So, it seems only natural that I have learned to cook several recipes where the main ingredient is ice cream. The best of these recipes come from the archives of Baskin-Robbins and were winners in the Baskin-Robbins Ice Cream Show-Off Recipe Contest (sort of like the Olympics of Fattening Foods).

Crushed Ice Cream Cone Pie is a snap to make and Peanut Brittle Fudge Squares are just so darned fattening, I couldn't resist including them in my book.

My two favorites, Turtle Pie and Grasshopper Pie, also both won Gold Medals at the California State Fair for two years running (1977 and 1978) and they both scored perfect marks—not one penalty. So, when Plain Jane tells you to "Go for the Gold," she doesn't mean to get out on the track—she means to serve up these Gold Medal Winners.

½ cup heavy cream
2 tablespoons banana liquor (optional)
1½ tablespoons confectioner's sugar
¼ cup Baskin-Robbins Hot Fudge Sauce
⅓ cup chunky peanut butter
1 pint Baskin-Robbins Banana ice cream
1 cup peanut brittle, crushed
1½ cups Baskin-Robbins Chocolate Chip ice cream

1. Whip cream until stiff peaks form.
2. Fold liquor and sugar into whipped cream and refrigerate.
3. Mix together hot fudge sauce and peanut butter.
4. Slightly soften banana ice cream and spread it evenly in a 8-inch square pan.

5. Mark out nine squares with a knife, then make an indentation with the back of a tablespoon in the center of each square.
6. Put about a tablespoon of the fudge/peanut butter mixture in each indentation, then sprinkle with about ½ cup of the crushed peanut brittle.
7. Spread the slightly softened chocolate chip ice cream over all of it, pressing down if necessary to make a smooth layer.
8. Put whipped cream on top and sprinkle on the rest of the crushed peanut brittle.
9. Freeze 3 hours until solid.
10. To serve, cut into squares. Makes 9 portions.

12 sugar cones, crushed
3 tablespoons almonds, chopped or slivered
6 ounces semisweet chocolate bits
2 tablespoons butter
1 quart Baskin-Robbins ice cream (choose your favorite flavor)

Crushed Ice Cream Cone Pie

1. Combine most of the crushed cones (put aside ¼ cup for later) with almonds.
2. Melt chocolate bits and butter and pour over cone mixture. Mix thoroughly until cones and nuts are well coated.
3. Press mixture into a 9-inch pie plate. Chill until firm.
4. Fill crust with quart (or more) of ice cream.
5. Sprinkle top with ¼ cup crushed cones that has been set aside.
6. Freeze well.

Dear Plain Jane,
    How can I remove a glob of gum from my favorite table cloth?

Emily C.
Lakeville, Conn.

Dear Emily,
    Scissors.

Jane

Grasshopper Pie

Crust:
1½ cups plus 1 tablespoon crushed chocolate cookies
½ cup melted butter

Filling:
11-ounce jar Baskin-Robbins Hot Fudge Sauce
1½ quarts Baskin-Robbins Chocolate Mint ice cream
1 can whipped dessert topping (or 1 cup chilled heavy cream whipped with ¼ cup confectioner's sugar)

1. Preheat oven to 375°.
2. To prepare crust, mix chocolate crumbs with butter.
3. With the back of a spoon, press mixture into the bottom and up the sides of a 9-inch pie plate.
4. Bake for 8 minutes, then remove to wire rack and cool completely. Freeze.
5. Spread 6 ounces of hot fudge sauce over the bottom (not the sides) of the frozen pie shell.
6. Take slightly softened ice cream and layer in overlapping sheets in pie plate. Press ice cream into place gently so that it is about ¼-inch below edge of pie crust and slightly mounded in center. Smooth surface.
7. Freeze the pie until solid (2 hours), then remove from freezer.
8. Drizzle remaining 5 ounces of hot fudge sauce across top to make crisscross design of latticework.
9. Make a fat border around edges of pie with whipped cream. Sprinkle remaining chocolate crumbs lightly on whipped cream.
10. Freeze until whipped cream is really frozen (about 2 hours).

Turtle Pie

Crust:
See recipe for crust of Grasshopper Pie above.

Filling:
¾ cup Baskin-Robbins Hot Fudge Sauce
1 quart Baskin-Robbins Pralines 'N' Cream™ ice cream

½ cup Baskin-Robbins Butterscotch Topping
8 pecan halves
¼ cup whipping cream, sweetened and whipped

1. Prepare crust as in Steps #1–#4 of Grass-hopper Pie.
2. Spread ½ cup hot fudge sauce in the bottom of prepared frozen pie shell. Freeze.
3. Spade thin sheets of ice cream on top of fudge. Smooth and slightly mound ice cream in center of pan.
4. Using the remainder of the fudge sauce, make a border around edge of pan with a spoon or use pastry bag with a #31 tip.
5. Drizzle butterscotch topping over ice cream and position pecan halves so that each slice will have a pecan in its center.
6. Place whipped cream in a spiral-shaped mound in the center of the pie.
7. Freeze until ready to serve.

1 22-ounce package Duncan Hines brownie
*   mix*
2 pints vanilla ice cream
2 cups sweetened whipped cream
Chocolate syrup

Brownie Ice Cream Loaf

1. Preheat oven to 350°.
2. Prepare brownie mix according to package.
3. Line a 13- × 9- × 2-inch pan with waxed paper and fill with batter.
4. Bake at 350° for 20 minutes. Cool for 10 minutes. Peel off paper and freeze brownie layer.
5. Cut brownie into three equal pieces (each 4 × 9 inches).
6. Place one piece of brownie on freezer-proof dish and top with thick layer of vanilla ice cream.
7. Top with second brownie and another layer of ice cream. (Note: Refreeze brownie if it starts to crumble when spreading ice cream.)
8. Top with third brownie layer.
9. Frost top and sides with whipped cream.
10. Freeze at least three hours. Serve with generous dose of chocolate syrup over each serving.

Reese's Pieces Ice Cream Saucers

LONG before they were being sold on every street corner in Manhattan, I had perfected the recipe for chocolate chip ice cream sandwiches. Only I made them the easy way—with Pillsbury refrigerated dough and Haagen-Dazs.

Now, I'm on to bigger and better things. Here's a recipe for chocolate/peanut butter cookies and ice cream. I won't be surprised to see someone hawking these Reese's Pieces Saucers on the corner of 38th and Madison tomorrow morning.

INGREDIENTS

½ cup shortening
1 cup sugar
1 egg
1 teaspoon vanilla
1½ cups plus 2 tablespoons all purpose, unsifted flour
⅓ cup unsweetened cocoa
½ teaspoon baking soda
½ teaspoon salt
¼ cup milk
1¼ cups Reese's Pieces
Ice cream (your favorite flavor)

1. Combine shortening, sugar, egg, and vanilla in a large mixing bowl until well blended.
2. Combine flour, cocoa, baking soda, and salt; add alternately with milk to mixture until ingredients are combined.
3. Chill about 1 hour.
4. Preheat oven to 375°.
5. Drop cookie dough by heaping tablespoons onto ungreased cookie sheet. Flatten each cookie with the palm of your hand or bottom of a glass into a 2½-inch circle about ¼ inch thick.
6. Evenly space 8 to 10 Reese's Pieces on the top of each cookie.
7. Bake at 375° for 8 to 10 minutes or until almost set.
8. Cool 1 minute on cookie sheet; remove to wire rack and cool completely.
9. Place scoop of slightly softened ice cream on flat side of one cookie and spread evenly with a spatula. Top with second cookie, pressing lightly.

Fashion Notes:
ACCESSORIZING WITH ALUMINUM FOIL

10. Wrap and immediately place in freezer. Freeze until firm. Makes about 12 4-inch ice cream sandwiches.

EMILY Perl Kingsley describes this as " . . . the gloppiest, gooiest, messiest, most fattening dessert I've ever made. It's also fabulously delicious and unusual. It's a knockout." I was convinced enough to try it and, honestly, Emily only underestimates this dessert.

By the way, although this recipe calls for 3 or 4 bananas, you can increase the ingredients to as many bananas as will fit in either your frying pan or chafing dish. As Emily says, "The more the better!"

3 or 4 bananas
Cinnamon
Nutmeg
Sugar
Butter
Grand Marnier
Butterscotch or caramel ice cream
Haagen-Dazs vanilla ice cream (or similar quality)

1. Slice bananas in half, lengthwise, and *leave the skin on.*
2. Sprinkle the cut side with spices and sugar and sauté, cut side down, in lots of butter.
3. Add a big splash of Grand Marnier and simmer a few seconds. Just before taking to the table (this can be done in a large chafing dish for a crowd) add a little more Grand Marnier and quickly light a match to it. Stir it around to keep the flame going. (Be careful!)
4. When flame has died, add a good amount of butterscotch or caramel ice cream and let it melt. Stir around to mix.
5. Lift off banana peels and cut bananas into pieces 1 inch to 1¼ inch.
6. Serve this gloppy delight over a good quality (and quantity) of vanilla ice cream.

Banana Flambé

INGREDIENTS

Candy Cooking

IT has been stated before but it is well worth repeating. The Plain Jane Philosophy of Cooking is to always make nine times the amount of food you think you'll need at any one given meal. Remember there's always Tupperware and freezers and that tomorrow is always another day for going off your diet.

This rule is especially true when you attempt to make any of the following candy recipes. I can't stress enough the importance of *quantity*. Remember that a sweet attack can happen at any time of the day or night.

Another thought to keep in mind is that homemade candy makes a lovely and thoughtful holiday gift for your family and friends. I would stress, however, another Plain Jane maxim, which is that it is not *always* more blessed to give than to receive (especially when the giving involves chocolate).

The Chocolate-Dipped Calvin Klein Strawberry

IF you're ever in the mood to serve fresh fruit for dessert, consider the appeal of the chocolate-dipped strawberry. It's almost as nutritious as fresh fruit and it tastes a whole lot better.

This recipe for chocolate-dipped strawberries has been laboriously perfected in my very own kitchen. I have named this dessert in honor of Calvin Klein because it's the best-dressed strawberry I've ever met.

A warning: I am going to get completely serious for this rest of this recipe because a great chocolate dessert is, really, no laughing matter.

Chocolate-dipped strawberries are relatively easy to make if you pay attention to the temperature and the handling of the chocolate. Although I don't usually get into specialty equipment, for this dessert I do recommend using a double boiler. A heating pad is optional.

INGREDIENTS

Strawberries—buy the biggest, freshest, most beautiful berries you can find.

Chocolate—you will need about 5 ounces of semisweet chocolate per pint of strawberries. Buy the best you can find: Tobler, Lindt, Michel

Guérard. **To save money, I combine one of these with ⅓ part Baker's Chocolate.**
Heavy sweet cream (whipped)
Raisins, nuts, coconut (for extra chocolate)

How to dip the Calvin Klein strawberry. NOTE: label is optional.

1. Wash the berries the night before preparing this dessert and allow at least 12 hours for them to air-dry. (Do not refrigerate.) It is essential that the berries be *absolutely dry*. Leave the stems and leaves intact.

2. Use a double boiler to melt the chocolate. Melt over barely simmering water and make sure that the water does not touch the top of the double boiler. Stir frequently.

3. Make certain that no water gets into the chocolate. Even a few drops of water from your spatula or steam from the double boiler can separate the chocolate beyond repair.

4. While dipping, replace the pan over simmering water every few minutes, but keep the flame of the heat very low. Do not allow any steam to build up on the pan while dipping and stir chocolate frequently. (An alternative method is to keep the top of the double boiler on a heated heating pad while dipping.)

5. Hold strawberry by the top stem and dip into pan. Cover three quarters of the strawberry with chocolate.

6. Place all the berries on waxed paper. If possible, balance the strawberry upside down, on its stem, to cool. If it won't balance, lay it on its side.

7. If you have any leftover chocolate, drop the nuts, raisins, or coconut (your choice) into the pan and stir. Remove in teaspoonful chunks and drop onto waxed paper. (Homemade raisinets are even better than the kind you buy at the movies.)

8. Do not refrigerate chocolate-dipped strawberries as they will sweat and the chocolate may crack. Leave them near an open window or other cool place. They will keep for about 24 hours.

Serve Calvin Klein strawberries with a dollop of whipped cream and a smile. Keep the raisinets for yourself.

IMPORTED DESSERT CHEESES

For your next party, serve a platter of imported cheeses for dessert.
Impress your guests with your continental-dessert savvy by serving a smattering
of cheeses from around the world:

English Cheddar

French Bonbel

Italian Blue

Greek Feta

Norwegian Jarlsberg

Danish Camembert

Philadelphia Cream

Lindsey's Bourbon Balls

MY friend Lindsey is known in several states for this delicious candy recipe. (However, contrary to common belief, her popularity during the Christmas season has nothing to do with the fact that she usually brings along a box of Bourbon Balls with every invitation.)

Because she's a gracious Southerner and a fellow writer, Lindsey has consented to allow me to reprint her infamous recipe. All she wants in return is a mention in this book. (Thank you, Lindsey Miller!)

The secret to this recipe is a basic rule of traditional Southern cooking, "When in doubt," Lindsey says, "spike it!" Personally, I have found this secret applies equally as well to Northern cooking, not to mention Eastern, Western, French, Italian, Mexican, Brazilian, Dutch, Russian, Spanish, Norwegian, and Eskimo cuisines.

Here's one recipe where I strongly advise you *not* to skimp on the ingredients—use a good bourbon and plenty of it. But be forewarned: Don't sample the ingredients too often or you'll never make it to that Christmas party.

2 cups vanilla wafers, crushed
1 cup confectioner's sugar
1 cup chopped walnuts or pecans
2 tablespoons good, unsweetened cocoa
2 tablespoons light corn syrup or honey
¼ cup, at least, good bourbon

INGREDIENTS

1. Mix all the ingredients together until moist but not soggy.
2. Roll by approximate teaspoonsful into little balls.
3. Roll the balls in more confectioner's sugar.

These are definitely grown-up treats. The kids will have to turn 18 (21 in some states) to enjoy these candies. Tell them it's worth the wait.

MARSHMALLOW Fluff should be a staple in everyone's pantry. You simply never know when you'll need to whip up a batch of Fluff Fudge.

Marshmallow Fluff Fudge

12 ounces semisweet chocolate
2 tablespoons sweet butter
1 can condensed milk
½ cup Marshmallow Fluff
½ cup miniature marshmallows
½ cup chopped walnuts

INGREDIENTS

1. In a double boiler, melt the butter and the chocolate.
2. Add the condensed milk, stirring constantly while cooking.
3. Turn off the heat and add the Marshmallow Fluff. Stir well.
4. Remove the pan from the heat; fold in the nuts and miniature marshmallows.
5. Pour mixture into a buttered 8-inch square pan and put into the refrigerator until well chilled.

Always store Fluff Fudge in the refrigerator—if there's anything left to store, that is.

Easy Peanut Butter Fudge

12-ounce package Reese's Peanut Butter Chips
14-ounce can sweetened condensed milk (not
*   evaporated)*
1 teaspoon vanilla

1. Line an 8-inch square pan with waxed paper.
2. Place peanut butter chips and sweetened condensed milk in top of double boiler over hot water.
3. Stir occasionally until chips melt and mixture is smooth.
4. Remove from heat; stir in vanilla.
5. Spread evenly in prepared pan.
6. Cover; chill 2 hours or until firm.
7. Peel off paper; cut into squares. Makes 1¼ pounds of fudge.

Aunt Mitzi's Chocolate-Peanut Delights

5½ cups of cornflakes
12-ounce bag of Hershey's semisweet chocolate bits
2 tablespoons peanut butter

1. Coarsely crush cornflakes.
2. In a double boiler, melt chocolate bits and add peanut butter. Stir until well blended and remove from heat.
3. Fold in cornflakes and cool slightly.
4. Make tablespoonful balls and place on a large cookie sheet. Freeze for half an hour.

If you enjoy cereal in the morning, try Aunt Mitzi's Delights with milk for breakfast. (Confidentally, I think that's why she makes them with cornflakes.)

AS children, we were taught the proper method for eating a package of Chuckles:
1) Tear open the cellophane with your teeth.
2) Throw away the Black Chuckle.
Well, now the time has come to pay the piper.

According to the latest government reports, we have run out of space for disposing of Black Chuckles.

Therefore, several environmental and ecological support groups have banded together to try to devise a practical application for these black, discarded candies *before it's too late*. This is no idle threat—if we can't come up with a workable solution to this problem, the Feds will be forced to halt the production of all Chuckles—yellows, reds, oranges, and greens alike.

We need your help. As a public service, I am calling upon any of my readers who can answer the question: What do you do with a Black Chuckle? Please send your responses to: The Black Chuckle Toxic Waste Dump, Route 5, Turnpike 8 at Highway 45, Mattahawan, N.J.

Please help if you can. Think about it: Do you want your kids growing up in a world without Chuckles?

A Public Service Message

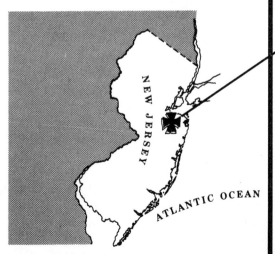

Location of the Black Chuckle Toxic Waste Dump

Appetizers

THE secret to serving great appetizers is twofold: 1) Make vast quantities of them and 2) Serve with gallons of vodka martinis. Remember that a totally soused guest will appreciate almost any kind of food.

The perfect appetizer recipe should be short, simple, and sweet. No appetizer recipe should take up more than ten lines on a file card. In addition, you should never have to share your best dip recipe with your friends.

Here, then, are Plain Jane's suggestions for truly fattening, truly delicious appetizers. Make as many as you can fit into your refrigerator and/or freezer. Appetizers rarely go to waste—you can always nibble on them after the guests have departed.

Cousin Betty's Vegetable Dip

Pat Grant's Green Dip

Easy Hot Artichoke Dip

Warm Clam Dip

Baked Clams

Cheryl's Best-Ever Sweet Appetizer

Bacon Things

Bubblin' Brown Sugar Bacon

My Sister's Mushroom Tarts

Evelyn Roselinsky's Blue Cheese Spread

Baked Brie

Bologna Barbecue

Hot Salami

Kielbasa

Cousin Betty's Vegetable Dip

THE farthest back I can trace this family recipe is to my mother's cousin Betty, who lives in North Miami Beach. (She's the same cousin Betty who refused to buy a copy of *Plain Jane Works Out*. She said she's waiting for me to send her an "autographed" copy. And I will—as soon as I get her check for $3.95, plus postage and handling, of course.)

Anyway, this dip is always a hit. For more than four guests, I usually double the ingredients. It makes a lot of dip but then I get to keep it in the refrigerator and nibble at it all week. (I can't, in all honesty, recommend freezing this dip. My mother's cousin Betty says she freezes it all the time, but I wouldn't take her word for it if I were you.)

INGREDIENTS

1 *10-ounce package frozen chopped spinach*
½ *8-ounce can water chestnuts*
1 *cup mayonnaise*
1 *cup sour cream*
1 *small onion*
1 *package Knorr's Vegetable Soup Mix (No substitutes!)*

1. Defrost spinach (use hot water, if necessary) and drain. Squeeze spinach tightly between your hands to remove as much water as possible.
2. Peel and chop onion.
3. Chop water chestnuts. (Onion and water chestnuts can be prepared in a food processor if, unlike me, you can use one of those machines without turning everything into mush.)
4. Mix together all the ingredients. Refrigerate at least one hour before serving.

I've named this dip after my mother's cousin Betty in the hopes that when Betty sees her name in this book, it will prompt her to actually buy her own copy.

Pat Grant's Green Dip

IT took an amazing amount of fast talking to weasel this recipe out of Pat. I could tell from the tone of her voice that she just didn't want to part with it. I think she might've been harboring thoughts of writing her own cookbook, calling it *Confessions of a Green Dip Queen*, and using this green dip recipe to launch the book. And you know what? It would've worked. This dip *is* a best-seller.

INGREDIENTS

1 *garlic clove*
8 *fresh spinach leaves or ½ bunch watercress leaves (no stems)*
1 *tablespoon chives (fresh, dried, or frozen)*
2 *tablespoons fresh parsley (don't use dried)*
2 or 3 *teaspoons dried dill or 2 tablespoons fresh dill*
8 *ounces cream cheese, softened (or whipped cream cheese)*
1 *tablespoon olive oil*

EATING IN BED:
Learn to chew food silently. Press lips tightly together and cover mouth with hand while chewing. Practice with M&Ms; when you feel more confident, graduate to pretzels.

1. In a blender or food processor, mince garlic clove.
2. Add spinach or watercress, chives, parsley, and dill. Process until well chopped.
3. Add cream cheese and olive oil. Process until the dip is well mixed and smooth.
4. Chill.

Pat Grant's Green Dip will remain fresh in the refrigerator for several weeks. Serve it with raw veggies or crackers. And let's all thank Pat for the contribution she's made to Plain Jane's royalty statement. Thanks, Pat!

Easy Hot Artichoke Dip

YOUR guests will think this appetizer took hours to prepare and that you must be a gourmet cook. Don't discourage this misconception.

INGREDIENTS

2 *cans of artichoke hearts, drained*
1 *cup fresh Parmesan cheese, grated*
1 *cup mayonnaise*

1 teaspoon garlic salt
Salt

1. Preheat oven to 350°.
2. In a blender, processor, or by hand, chop arti-chokes and combine with other ingredients.
3. Spoon into an oven-proof glass dish. Sprinkle with salt and more cheese.
4. Bake at 350° for 25 minutes. Serve hot with bread or crackers.

1 10-ounce can whole baby clams
⅓ cup mayonnaise
8 ounces cream cheese
1 or 2 cloves crushed garlic, to taste

Warm Clam Dip

1. Preheat oven to 300°.
2. Take 2 tablespoons of clam juice and pour over the mayo and cream cheese. Mix until smooth.
3. Add garlic. Drain clams, discard liquid, and fold clams into cheese mixture.
4. Put into a baking dish and heat at 300° for 15 to 20 minutes or until hot.

Serve warm with Doritos. If there's any leftover dip, it's also great to serve cold or to use for Bacon Things (see recipe on pg. 71.)

2 6½-ounce cans minced clams, drained
2 sticks melted butter
1½ cups crushed Ritz crackers
4 tablespoons Parmesan cheese, grated
½ cup flavored bread crumbs
2 teaspoons oregano
1 grated onion

Baked Clams

1. Preheat oven to 350°.
2. Blend all ingredients.
3. Pour into individual seashells or small alumi-num cups (about 6 to 8) or a casserole.
4. Bake at 350° for 30 minutes.

Cheryl's Best-Ever Sweet Appetizer

How to prepare logs

AT every party, there's one appetizer that disappears long before any of the others and, usually, leaves your guests begging for the recipe. This is the one.

In several parts of New Jersey, this recipe made Cheryl famous as the best source for party appetizers. Lucky for me (and you) Cheryl happens to be my sister's best friend.

I called my sister for this recipe. "The recipe is meant to serve four," Susan said over the phone. "But write that you should make about nine times what you think you'll need." That, in a nutshell, tells you how good this recipe is and, more to the point, succinctly summarizes the Plain Jane Philosophy of Cooking. In one word, Golden Rule Number One is: QUANTITY, QUANTITY, QUANTITY.

INGREDIENTS

8 slices white bread
1 8-ounce package cream cheese
1 teaspoon vanilla
1 egg yolk
2 tablespoons sugar
¼ pound sweet butter, melted
1 cup sugar
1 teaspoon cinnamon
1 pint sour cream

1. Preheat oven to 350°.
2. Remove crust and roll bread thin.
3. Blend together cream cheese, vanilla, egg yolk, and sugar.
4. Spread mixture on bread and roll bread into a log.
5. Dip the log into butter and roll in sugar and cinnamon.
6. Cut each log into 3 pieces and put on a cookie sheet. (At this point you can freeze the logs. When you want to serve them, thaw for 10 minutes before baking.)
7. Bake at 350° for 5 to 10 minutes.

Serve with sour cream for dipping and stand clear of the stampede.

Bacon Things

I don't know whom to credit for this recipe because it actually came from two different friends. One lives in Boston, the other in New York and, no, they don't know each other.

Jean invented the name, Bacon Things, but the Boursin (a stroke of genius) was Doe's idea.

You'll have to adjust the following ingredients to the number and the appetite-quotient of your guests. Use your best judgment and figure that each slice of bread makes four (smallish) pieces.

INGREDIENTS

Pepperidge Farm White Bread (or other thin-sliced white bread, although Doe insists on Pepperidge Farm, only)
Boursin cheese (or any cream-cheese-based cheese) or use Clam Dip (see recipe on pg. 69)
Bacon slices

1. Preheat oven to 350°.
2. Cut crusts from bread and roll thin.
3. Spread with Boursin (*or* other cheese *or* dip) and roll into a log. (See illustration on pg. 70.)
4. Cut each log into four pieces and wrap each one in a piece of raw bacon. Secure with toothpick.
5. Bake in 350° oven for 20 minutes or until bacon is crisp. Serve at once.

When serving, be sure to remind your guests to remove the toothpicks before swallowing Bacon Things.

Bubblin' Brown Sugar Bacon

COAT strips of bacon with lots of brown sugar and place on a cookie sheet. Bake in a 325° oven for 45 minutes or until brown sugar bubbles. Serve hot as appetizer.

Dear Plain Jane,
At the grocery store, I recently found a bag of shrunken Snickers candy bars.
What is the purpose of these bite-sized candies?
Mabel L.
Mobile, Ala.

Dear Mabel from Mobile,
This is called progress. Like the computer chip, Snickers have been miniaturized.
However, these teeny, tiny candy bars do serve an important function: they can easily be hidden in your pockets, purses, shirt sleeves, and undergarments.
Jane

My Sister's Mushroom Tarts

THESE are not the easiest appetizers to make—but I suppose they're not the hardest either.

This is my sister Susan's recipe and it's really delicious. It's also about as close as I'll ever come to making a scratch crust for any dish. In order to make these tarts, I actually had to go out and purchase a rolling pin.

Truthfully, I didn't mind buying the rolling pin (it made me feel like a real baker), but I do mind having to store it in my kitchen—it just doesn't fit in anywhere. The rolling pin is too large for the drawer, too unstable for a cabinet, and it doesn't have a hook or handle for hanging. Therefore, I have to store it sort of half-in and half-out of an open shelf. Considering that I only use it once a year, I certainly have to look at it a lot.

Has any one of my readers come up with a better storage plan for their rolling pins? If so, please let me know before mine rolls off the shelf and onto my foot, again.

INGREDIENTS

Crust:
3 3-ounce packages cream cheese
½ cup soft butter
1½ cups flour

·Filling:
1 small minced onion

4 teaspoons butter
2 cups mushrooms, coarsely chopped
½ cup sour cream
Salt
Pepper
Thyme
4 teaspoons flour

1. Preheat oven to 450°.
2. Mix together cream cheese and butter.
3. Add 1½ cups flour and work into dough. Refrigerate for 45 minutes.
4. Meanwhile, sauté onion in butter and add mushrooms.
5. Stir in sour cream, salt, pepper, and thyme and set aside.
6. Roll dough very thin on a floured surface and use the rim of a 3-inch glass to cut out rounds.
7. Fill each round with about ½ teaspoon of filling, fold and seal edges like a turnover. Pinch sides all around.
8. Prick each tart with a fork. Bake in a 450° oven for 15 minutes or until brown.

You can prepare these tarts the night before serving, but don't freeze them.

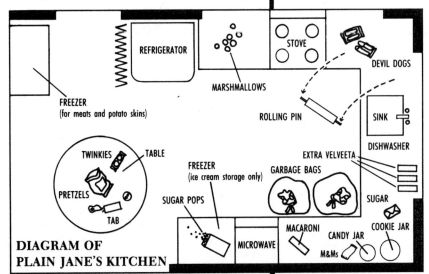

REFRIGERATOR

STOVE

DEVIL DOGS

MARSHMALLOWS

FREEZER
(for meats and potato skins)

ROLLING PIN

SINK

DISHWASHER

TWINKIES

TABLE

EXTRA VELVEETA

FREEZER
(ice cream storage only)

GARBAGE BAGS

PRETZELS

SUGAR POPS

SUGAR

TAB

MICROWAVE

MACARONI

CANDY JAR

COOKIE JAR

M&Ms

**DIAGRAM OF
PLAIN JANE'S KITCHEN**

Evelyn Roselinsky's Blue Cheese Spread

THIS recipe comes from Lynn's mother. Lynn and I went to high school together and my fondest memories of Mrs. Roselinsky are when she'd quit smoking and insist that I light a cigarette and blow the smoke in her direction. As far as I can recall, Mrs. Roselinsky quit smoking every other week during my junior and senior year in high school.

Mr. and Mrs. Roselinsky now live in Florida where appetizers and cocktails are the main course of the day. This is one of Evelyn's favorite cheese appetizers.

INGREDIENTS

4 ounces blue cheese
8 ounces cream cheese
½ stick butter
1 small onion, grated
Worcestershire sauce
Black pitted olives, sliced

1. Soften cheeses to room temperature and mix well with other ingredients.
2. Shape into ball and refrigerate.
3. Soften to room temperature before serving.

Baked Brie

PLACE a quarter, half, or full wheel of brie in an oven-proof serving dish and bake in a 325° oven until the cheese starts to melt. Serve warm with crackers. (You can try this with other brick cheeses also.)

Bologna Barbecue

IN a blender, combine 1 cup of apricot preserves, 6 tablespoons of Dijon mustard, and ⅓ cup apricot liquor. Slash ¼-inch cuts in 2 whole bologna and baste with sauce. Grill over barbecue. Cut into small pieces and serve with toothpicks. (Also try this method with salami.)

Dear Plain Jane,
Why do I always cry when I peel onions?
Talia K.
Dallas, Tx.

Dear Talia,
You cry when peeling onions for a very simple reason. Like me, you hate doing menial chores. The best remedy for crying when peeling onions is to hire a cook to do it for you.
Plain Jane

Hot Salami

COAT a salami with your favorite mustard and place in an oven-proof serving dish. Bake at 350° for about 30 to 40 minutes. Slice and serve warm with crackers.

Kielbasa

KIELBASA is a Polish sausage that tastes great even if you don't like sausages. Here's three different ways of serving it as an appetizer.

1 1-pound kielbasa
2 or 3 small onions
¼ cup water
½ cup white wine or vermouth
Butter

1. Slice kielbasa and then slice onions.
2. Fry onions and kielbasa in the water and liquor.
3. When liquid evaporates, brown kielbasa and onions in butter. Serve with toothpicks.

Variation: Use a 12-ounce bottle of beer instead of the water and liquor and follow the directions above.

Variation: Barbecue a whole kielbasa. Slice and serve with different mustards.

Snacks

QUITE often I am asked: How many snacks, per day, should one person consume?

The only way to answer this question is to break it down into component questions such as: How many snacks, per afternoon, should I consume? How many snacks, per hour, should I consume? And, even more relevant: How many snacks, per 15-minute intervals, should I consume?

Even in their most basic form, these are difficult questions to assess. Studies have shown that everyone has their own Personal Snack Potential (PSP, for short).

Currently, I am trying to cut my PSP to a ratio of $\frac{1}{30}$ which, in lay terms, translates to the following equation: $\frac{1\ \text{Twinkie Per}}{30\ \text{minutes}}$. Of course, I am not always successful with such severe restrictions. But, at least I try (sometimes).

Snack Suggestions

Fluffernutter: The Singing Snack

Marshmallow Popcorn

Adding Calories to Hot-Air Popcorn

S'Mores

Avocado Melt

THE following list represents my recommendations for snacks (other than those included in the recipes in the book).

Choose one of the following or combine several items. Be creative!

Remember that proper snacking is almost like proper eating.

Snack Suggestions

Hostess Cup Cakes

Bubble Gum in a tube

Wonder Bread squished into a ball

Twinkies

Bonomo Turkish Taffy

Chicken in a Biskit Crackers

Devil Dogs

Wise Potato Chips

Welch's Grape Juice

Kool-Aid crystals (with or without water)

Mayo on white bread

Bullwinkle Chocolate Pops

Animal Crackers

Mayo on anything

Handful of Sugar Pops

Dollop of Reddi-Wip

Sugar Babies

Fritos Corn Chips

Doritos Nacho Chips

Beefaroni

Frozen Milky Ways

Room temperature Milky Ways

Semimelted Milky Ways

Liquid Milky Ways

Yoo-Hoo

SNACKING:

Remember that it is best to snack only *between* meals, never during dinner or between courses.

Cocoa Puffs

Yodels

Cheese (plain or aerosol)

Super Sugar Crisp Cereal

Dunkin' Donuts

Any kind of donut

A slab of Velveeta

Hawaiian Punch

Spaghetti-o's

Beef Jerky

Milk Duds

Fudgsicles

Fiddle Faddle

Ding Dongs

Snickers

Anything leftover from yesterday

Life Savers

Good 'N' Plenty

Popsicles

Baby Ruths

Sprinkles

Tootsie Rolls

Pepperidge Farm Goldfish

Several strands of cold spaghetti

Goobers

Spoonful of Marshmallow Fluff

Popcorn: any flavor

Jujubes

Sugar buttons on paper

Nuts (any kind)

Chef Boy–Ar–Dee Ravioli

Dots

Cool Whip

Barbecued potato chips

M&Ms

Reese's Pieces

Marshmallows (plain or roasted)

Hotdogs (plain or roasted)

Pizza (fresh, frozen, reheated, or cold)

Ice cream

Ice cream

Ice cream

SNACK TIMETABLE

Snack #1—6:30 AM to 8:30 AM (or anytime before breakfast)
Cheese danish or donut or both (just to tide me over until breakfast)

Breakfast

Snack #2—10:30 AM to 11:30 AM
Coffee, coffee, coffee, with cream, sugar, and coffee cake

Snack #3—11:30 AM to 12:00 NOON
Cold Chinese food from last night's take-out dinner

Lunch

Snack #4—2:30 PM to 3:00 PM
Fresh fruit with a pound of Cheez Whiz, Screaming Yellow Zonkers, Nacho Chips

Snack #5—4:00 PM to 5:00 PM
Popcorn, Cracker Jack, Hot dog

Snack #6—6:00 PM to 6:30 PM
Assorted appetizers

Dinner

Snack #7—8:00 PM to bedtime
Anything not nailed down in my refrigerator

Snack #8—3:00 AM (or whenever I wake up in the middle of the night)
Anything left over from Snack #7

The Fluffernutter:* A Singing Snack

* © 1961 Durkee-Mower

MICHAEL Uslan and I were having lunch in a posh Manhattan restaurant when I made the mistake of asking him for a recipe for my new cookbook. "Fluffernutters!" he exclaimed and proceeded to sing (loudly) the following jingle. I tried to look nonchalant as the waiter glanced quizzically at our table. Well, I should've known this would happen—Michael is in the middle of writing a trivia quiz book on television commercials.

See if you can sing along with the Fluffernutter song. (The jingle is the recipe.)

Oh, you need Fluff, Fluff, Fluff
To make a "Fluffernutter."
Marshmallow Fluff
And lots of peanut butter.
First you spread, spread, spread
Your bread with peanut butter.
Add Marshmallow Fluff,
And have a Fluffernutter.
Oh, you'll enjoy, joy, joy
Your bread with peanut butter
You'll be glad to have enough
For another Fluffernutter.

The beauty of Fluffernutters is that they contain 100% of your daily minimum allowance for glucose, sucrose, and dextrose.

"But," Michael added, "warn your readers not to operate heavy machinery after eating one of these Fluffers."

Marshmallow Popcorn

¼ stick butter
4 cups miniature marshmallows
Popcorn, popped

Melt butter and marshmallows over low heat, stirring constantly. Pour over popcorn and stir with wooden spoon. Drop on waxed paper or mold into shapes.

POPCORN is very dietetic when popped in a hot-air machine without using any oil or salt. This method is actually recommended as a snack on many diet plans.

Once, when I was on a diet (which lasted well into the afternoon) I tried hot-air popcorn and, I admit, I rather liked it. And I felt good knowing I had limited my intake of salt and oil.

My throat got a little dry, however, after the fourth or fifth batch so I decided to compensate for the lack of grease and seasoning by adding cheese.

Adding Calories to Hot-Air Popcorn

1. Pop a pound of popcorn, roughly the equivalent bulk of two large pillowcases (king size).
2. Add small chunks of your favorite hard cheese. I prefer muenster but cheddar and Jarlsberg also work nicely. Or, sprinkle generously with Parmesan cheese. (None of the cheeses will melt, but they do get nice and warm.)
3. Serve with several buckets of soda.

One graham cracker
One marshmallow
One chunk of chocolate

S'mores

On a graham cracker, place one marshmallow and top with chocolate. Heat in a toaster oven until the marshmallow and the chocolate are melted. Enjoy!

Culinary Footnote: In the South, S'mores are called Moon Pies and, served with chilled RC Cola, they represent the regional junk food in seven southern states.

MELT a thick slice of Stilton (or your choice) cheese over half an avocado. This is better than a melted cheese sandwich because an avocado is a lot richer (and far more fattening) than any slice of bread.

Avocado Melt

Entrees

AT most dinner parties, I would prefer to skip the main course altogether. I have found, however, that every time I have people over for dinner, they expect to be served *something* between the soup and the soufflé. Therefore, I have been forced to accumulate a smattering of decent main courses.

Main courses are too basic to be really interesting but there are ways to jazz up your entrees. For instance, I have found that, in most cases, a pint of sour cream will do wonders for any chicken dish, ketchup will greatly enhance red meat, and heavy cream always tastes great on pasta.

Chicken Marcella

Tofu and Chicken Supreme

Chicken in Rum Crumbs

Plain Jane Chicken Magnificent

Chicken Marinade

Duck à l'Orange (or Apricot) Sunshine

My Ex-Stockbroker's Brisket

Doe's Quiches

Blintz Soufflé

My Brother-in-Law's French Toast

Two Macaroni and Cheese Recipes

Washington-to-New York Lasagna

Eggplant Parmigiana with Smoked Mozzarella

Plain Jane Pesto for Pasta

Plain Jane Pasta Cream Sauce

Chicken Marcella

THIS recipe comes, originally, from Marcella's ex-mother-in-law and is, I think, the most positive thing I ever heard Marcella say about her entire marriage. (Well, never mind, many of my other divorced friends have come out of their marriages with a lot less than one great chicken recipe.)

Quite by accident, Marcella improved on her mother-in-law's recipe one evening, when she inadvertently picked up the cinnamon instead of the paprika. So, to use the correct amount of cinnamon in this recipe, you should really dump a tablespoon of it into the sour cream, scream twice and then carefully scrape out as much of the spice as you can. Or, you can simply use your best judgment and try to estimate the equivalent of such a procedure.

6 chicken thighs (or use chicken breasts)
Garlic powder
Salt (to taste)
1 tablespoon paprika
3 medium-sized onions, sliced
Butter
1 bouillon cube dissolved in 1 cup hot water
½ cup sour cream
Dash of cinnamon
Rice

INGREDIENTS

1. Season chicken with garlic, salt, and a dash of the paprika (for color).
2. Quickly sear the chicken in a hot frying pan or electric skillet. Sear both sides in oil and remove from pan.
3. Sauté sliced onions in butter until slightly limp but not too soft.
4. Put chicken in pan and sauté on both sides.
5. Add the cup of chicken broth and let simmer for 20 minutes.
6. Remove the chicken from the pan and set aside. Add the sour cream to the onions, stirring constantly to avoid any lumps.
7. Add the paprika and then a tiny dash of cinnamon. Continue to stir constantly for 5 minutes.
8. Return the chicken to the pan and simmer

for 20 minutes, turning the chicken once after the first 10 minutes. Meanwhile, prepare the rice.

Serve with the rice. Try not to let this dish remind you of your own divorce. If anything, keep in mind that, after the divorce, you'll never again have to cook for your in-laws.

Tofu and Chicken Supreme

FOR the sake of my health-conscious readers, I am including this traditional dinner recipe.

As my readers know, I am a proponent of the High-Salt, High-Sugar, High-Fat, Hi-Mom, Hi-Pop, Hy Tarnower Diet. I am, after all, a product of my childhood.

When I was a kid, I used to beg my mother for sweets. I didn't want to eat my spinach, I wanted to go straight to dessert. But, no, my mother would hold out the Hostess Cup Cakes until all the green had vanished from my plate.

"Just wait till I grow up," I'd mutter to myself. "My daughter will never have to eat all this green glob—I'll let my kids eat hot dogs and candy at every meal."

My mother would flash her Cheshire Cat grin. (I figured she was smiling because she could eat all the cup cakes she wanted.) Little did I know, back then, what fate would have in store for me.

Today, I have a lovely family all my own—a beautiful daughter I can torture by withholding sweets in the same manner in which my mother trained me.

But does *my* little girl give me the satisfaction I gave to my mother? Of course not. Bless her prepubescent heart, my little Janey Junior is a vegetarian. She doesn't beg for hamburgers or Hostess, she only wants spinach.

Currently, Janey's on some kind of macro/micro/antibiotic diet, constantly complaining about my apparently unsavory eating habits. To satisfy her in the same tradition I learned in my mother's kitchen, I serve this recipe for Tofu and Chicken Supreme.

Frankly, I've grown to love this meal. I like to serve it after a long, hard day when my nerves are particularly frazzled. I find that the all-natural ingredients and the ease of preparation helps to relax me and it does seem to put the entire family into a state of pure nirvana. Maybe there is something to his health-food craze after all. Maybe we should listen to our children when they suggest new ways of eating and looking at the world.

So, the next time your little darling calls you a "prehistoric, meat-eating barbarian," just smile like a Cheshire Cat and serve up Tofu and Chicken Supreme.

INGREDIENTS

Tofu
Chicken
Telephone
Wine

1. Throw out the tofu.
2. Call Colonel Sanders and order a bucket to go.
3. Drink the wine.

HERBS: Medicinal Properties

For centuries, herbs have been used to cure and heal. Listed below are a few of the more readily available herbs and their curative properties.

Alfalfa: Partner of Spanky.

Camomile: Movie starring Greta Garbo.

Cumin: The door's open.

Ginger: Danced with Fred.

Marjoram: Morningstar.

Peppermint: Patty.

Rosemary: Clooney.

Thyme: To turn the page.

Chicken in Rum Crumbs

I'M basically for any recipe that will fatten up boring old chicken. So, when Pat told me about chicken in rum and bread crumbs, I listened with pen in hand.

I figured this recipe had to be great—it's made with alcohol and bread crumbs—two of my favorite ingredients.

INGREDIENTS

4 chicken breasts, boned, skinned, and split
4 tablespoons chutney, chopped fine
1½ cups fine, fresh bread crumbs
½ cup Myers's dark rum
Clarified butter for browning
Salt and pepper to taste

1. Preheat oven to 350°.
2. Pound chicken breasts between two pieces of waxed paper.
3. Mix chutney with a few bread crumbs and 1 tablespoon of the rum.
4. Making sure the outside of the breast is the smooth side, put a spoonful of the mixture on each breast and roll up like a envelope (fold sides in, then top and bottom over). Secure with toothpicks.

5. Dip in rum and then crumbs.
6. Brown each piece in butter and place in shallow baking dish. Sprinkle some extra crumbs on top, then dribble some butter over the top.
7. Sprinkle with salt and pepper.
8. Bake uncovered in a 350° oven for 15 to 18 minutes or until firm to the touch. Do not overcook.

Plain Jane Chicken Magnificent

1 bottle Italian or Caesar salad dressing
Proscuitto slices
Smoked mozzarella or other favorite cheese
Chicken breasts, boned, skinned and split
Bread crumbs

1. Marinate chicken breasts in salad dressing, overnight in refrigerator, if possible.
2. Preheat oven to 350°.
3. Cut each breast in half and pound thin.
4. Place a slice of proscuitto (or several slices) and a slice of cheese over each breast.
5. Roll breast and fold in edges. Secure with toothpick. (Note: Cheese and ham are rolled up inside chicken. Rolling chicken is never easy, so don't feel badly if you have to use several toothpicks.)
6. Dip in bread crumbs.
7. Bake in shallow pan at 350° for 25 to 30 minutes or until done.

Dear Plain Jane,
   After publishing *Plain Jane Works Out*, did you ever hear from Jane Fonda?

Naomi
Nome, Alaska

Dear Naomi from Nome,
   Did I hear from her? Naomi, the woman has not stopped calling since the day my book was published.
   First, she just wanted to congratulate me but now she acts as though she's my best friend—she wants advice, endorsements, encouragement, you name it.
   I don't mean to complain, really I don't. I'm flattered by all her attention but I'm also a very busy woman and I simply don't have the time to help Jane Fonda solve every little problem that comes up in her life. And, anyway, what do I know about option deals and approval clauses?
   But what can I do? I mean, the woman is a major motion picture star and I can't just ignore her.
   I only wish that once, just once, she'd call first before dropping over for the weekend with all of her Hollywood friends.

Plain Jane

Chicken Marinade

INGREDIENTS

DOE invented this marinade for chicken but it works equally as well for lamb or steak (especially London broil).

½ cup olive oil
½ cup soy sauce
2 tablespoons chopped ginger or scallions

1. Mix liquids with whisk and add ginger or scallions.
2. Marinate meat for several hours before broiling and save sauce for use with baked potato and sour cream.

Use this marinade when you barbecue too.

Duck à l'Orange (or Apricot) Sunshine

INGREDIENTS

NO matter how many packages of stuffing, pints of sour cream, boxes of bread crumbs, or cans of cream of mushroom soup you use, you'll never be able to make chicken as fattening as duck.

Because of its insulated layers of fat, duck is simply a much more fattening fowl than chicken could ever aspire to be.

On top of this fact, my mother adds a 10,000 calorie marinade to her roast duck. And then she'll serve it with noodle pudding (see recipe on pg. 12.) Is it any wonder that I grew up to write this book?

1 fresh duckling (3 or 4 pounds)
4 medium-sized onions
Kosher salt

Marinade:
1 bottle 1891 Salad Dressing (or any similar
    sweet and sour French dressing)
1 package onion soup mix
½ jar orange marmalade or apricot preserves
    (your preference)
½ cup orange juice

1. Preheat oven to 400°.

2. Clean duckling and rub all over with kosher salt, inside and outside cavity.
3. Peel and cut onions in half and place in cavity.
4. Place duck on rack in roasting pan and put in oven.
5. The onions and salt will render the fat, which you will have to keep removing until duck is really dried out, about 1½ hours.
6. Remove and place duck on brown paper. When slightly cooled, cut with poultry shears into 8 pieces and set aside.
7. Mix marinade ingredients in a saucepan over low heat until thoroughly blended (about 5 minutes.)
8. Drench duck in marinade and refrigerate in a covered oven-proof casserole for 3 to 4 hours but preferably overnight.
9. Before serving, bake in hot oven for one hour and then broil 10 minutes for extra crispness.

My Ex-Stockbroker's Brisket

HE'S no longer my broker so he will go nameless, but I can tell you that he's a better cook than he was a broker.

He once gave me this terrific recipe for brisket made with gingersnaps and it's the only thing I have left from our business association except for one hot tip: don't play the stock market.

INGREDIENTS

1 brisket (sized to number of people)
Paprika
Garlic powder
Salt
Pepper
4 onions, sliced
10 gingersnaps, broken

1. Preheat oven to 325°.
2. Season brisket with spices and cover with sliced onions.
3. Cover pan and put in 325° oven for 1 hour.
4. Turn brisket over and swish in ginger snaps. Cook, covered, for another hour.

Menu Planning on 13,000 Calories a Day: Ethnic Meals

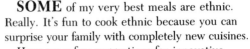

SOME of my very best meals are ethnic. Really. It's fun to cook ethnic because you can surprise your family with completely new cuisines.

Here are a few suggestions for innovative meals based upon my very favorite ethnics:

The Perfect French Dinner
1. Lots of French bread and butter
2. French fries
3. Pie à la mode

The Perfect Italian Dinner
1. Lots of Italian bread and butter
2. Pizza, pizza, pizza
3. Pasta, pasta, pasta
4. Thirteen pounds of those little Italian pastries

The Perfect American Dinner
1. Hot dogs
2. Peanuts
3. Cotton candy
4. Corn on the cob
5. Ice cream
6. Apple pie
7. Coke
8. Something chocolate
9. Stomach pump

The Perfect Indian Dinner
1. Popcorn
2. Popcorn
3. Popcorn
4. Tab (not strictly Navaho, but you'll need something to wash down all that popcorn)

The Perfect Midwest Dinner
1. Spam
2. White bread
3. Ritz crackers
4. Ketchup
5. Tang

The Perfect Vegetarian Dinner
1. Lots of whole wheat bread and butter
2. Pasta, pasta, pasta
3. Carrot cake

The Perfect Blue Dinner
1. Blue Cheese
2. Blue Bonnet margarine
3. Veal Cordon Bleu
4. Blueberry tart
5. Blue Nun wine
6. True Blue cigarettes

The Perfect Frozen Dinner
1. Chicken pot pie
2. Buttermilk biscuits
3. Haagen-Dazs

The Perfect Dinner
1. Three pounds of Oreos
2. A quart of cold milk
3. A Bette Davis movie

Dear Plain Jane,
    Help! Next month I have to serve a sit-down dinner for 10 (!) of my husband's clients. I have never served anything more fancy than ice cream and pin-the-tail-on-the-donkey. What can I do?
                           Panicked in Pittsburg

Dear Panicked,
    You've got a real problem there, all right. I'm no expert on sit-down parties, so I went to the mother of all party problems and consulted THE JOY OF COOKING by Irma Rombauer.
    Irma offers the following advice:
    1) Your cook can double as a waitress.
    2) Your well-behaved children can be trained to assist in table clearing and food presentation.
    I hope this is helpful.
                                Jane

Doe's Quiches

MYSELF, I never went too heavily into quiche. Not that I had anything against the dish, but to me quiche was nothing more than scrambled eggs in a pie crust.

All that changed, however, at a recent office party when the multitalented vice-president, Doe Coover, surprised us with two of her homemade quiches. Now, *these* pies were the best I'd ever tasted, a whole new culinary sensation, and I'm not just saying that because Doe is the one who approves my expense account. Really, that fact has nothing whatsoever to do with the praise I lavish on this quiche recipe. (Look, I know my dinner expenses for the week ending May 12th were slightly extravagant but, Doe, really, you do make the best quiche in all of the greater Boston area. Honest.)

INGREDIENTS

Crust:
Pillsbury pie crust (from your grocer's dairy)

Filling:
5 eggs
8 ounces heavy cream
Salt
Pepper

Choose *one* of the following combinations:
8 ounces Roquefort cheese
½ cup walnuts
1 cup broccoli (steamed and cut into small pieces)

or

½ cup pepperoni
½ cup tomato and scallions (dejuice tomatoes—cut, salt, and drain)
8 ounces mixture of provolone and mozzarella cheeses
2 tablespoons Parmesan cheese, grated

or

10 medium shrimp (cooked and cut in half)
6 stalks asparagus (cooked and cut into 2-inch pieces)
8 ounces Swiss or Gruyère or combine both

2 tablespoons Parmesan cheese, grated

1. Preheat oven to 375°.
2. Roll out the pie crust a little bit bigger than a 10-inch pie dish. Line dish with pastry.
3. The heavy ingredients go in first—depending on the combination you choose—place vegetables, meat, or shrimp in dish.
4. Add cheeses (but hold Parmesan).
5. Add Parmesan.
6. In a separate bowl, thoroughly mix the cream and eggs and add to dish.
7. Sprinkle top with nutmeg for Roquefort or shrimp; basil and oregano for pepperoni.
8. Bake in preheated 375° oven for 45 minutes to 1 hour or until a toothpick comes out clean.
9. Cool for 15 minutes before serving.

This recipe seems long because it actually covers three different quiches. It's really quite simple to follow.

According to Doe, the secret to this recipe is *not* to use too much of the vegetables or meats for the filling. It's true that our tendency is always to add a little extra but, in this case, the veggies exude moisture and any more than the recommended amounts will make your quiches watery, runny, and generally yucky. So, take a tip from an expert and remember that sometimes (but not often) less is better.

G REAT WINES
ON TIGHT BUDGET

Night Train

Mogen David

Champale

Thunderbird

Wine Vinegar

PLAIN JANE'S SEASONAL HOLIDAY FOOD CHECKLIST

ST. PATRICK'S DAY	Corned Beef & Cabbage
EASTER	Hardboiled Eggs
FOURTH OF JULY	Hot Dogs
MOTHER'S DAY	Apple Pie
HALLOWEEN	Snickers
THANKSGIVING	Turkey
CHRISTMAS	Roasted Chestnuts

Blintz Souffle

A Blintz by any
other name would be called:

A crêpe (French)

An egg roll (Chinese)

A cannelloni or ravioli
(Italian)

A blini (Russian)

An enchilada (Mexican)

Teki-maki (Japanese)

INGREDIENTS

MY editor advises me to define a "blintz" before giving the recipe for this dish. He says that there are people in this world who've never heard of a blintz. Can that possibly be true? Well, for you unfortunate souls, let me define a blintz by saying you start with a dollop of something fattening (like cheese or sugared fruit) and then you wrap that up in something equally as fattening (like a pancake). A blintz is really an ethnic crêpe and, like crêpes, they are not easy to prepare.

For this recipe you will need a dozen blintzes. You can prepare the blintz like my grandmother did in the Old Country where blintz-making was something of an art.

If, on the other hand, you do not have an extra day or two to handmake the blintzes, you can Americanize the preparations in true Plain Jane style.

First, go directly to your grocer's freezer. (Listen, what they don't know in the Old Country could fill a cookbook.) Second, buy two packages of frozen blintzes—either cheese, blueberry, or cherry. (Conveniently, they come six to a package.)

The next step for this recipe is to add the soufflé part. Now, you've really doubled your pleasure. Sure, it's doubly as fattening but look on the bright side—it's not illegal or immoral (although it's much better than most things that are.)

2 packages of frozen blintzes (12), fruit or cheese
¼ cup sugar
½ teaspoon vanilla
1 pint sour cream
6 eggs
½ stick sweet butter

1. Preheat oven to 350°.
2. Place blintzes in buttered fitted oven-proof dish.
3. Mix sugar, vanilla, sour cream, eggs, and butter.
4. Pour mixture over blintzes.
5. Bake at 350° for 45 minutes to 1 hour (until bubbling).

I can't decide if this dish is better as a main course or dessert. (It makes a perfect brunch dish.) For best results, serve as both and decide for yourself.

Dear Plain Jane,
I'm five months pregnant and my doctor says I must drink a quart of milk a day. Ugh! I hate milk. What can I do?

Barefoot and Preggers
Park Slope, N.Y.

Dear Barefoot in the Park,
Pregnancy is the most wonderful time in a woman's life because you can eat *anything* you want.
And, of course, you must drink gallons of milk but if you don't like plain milk try chocolate milk, Ovaltine, and/or milk shakes.
Remember that everyone expects you to get fat—so don't disappoint them.

Jane

I am including this breakfast recipe because, aside from barbecueing, it's the only cooking my brother-in-law does. However, I have discovered that Peter's French toast is worth the enormous effort it takes to cajole him into making it.

Peter has five secrets to making French toast and here are all of them:

1. Use a thick slab of bread, white or challah, that you have cut from a solid loaf of bread.
2. Add a dash of vanilla extract to the eggs-and-milk batter.
3. Pierce the bread to allow eggs and milk to really soak through.
4. Fry in lots of butter and serve with a thick coating of sugar.
5. Insist that your wife (or sister-in-law) clean up the kitchen when you're done cooking.

My Brother-in-Law's French Toast

Two Macaroni and Cheese Recipes

I couldn't decide which of these recipes was better, so I am giving you both of them. I think that Vicki's is a little more fattening (but Susan's is made with Velveeta and I simply had to include a Velveeta recipe in my book).

Susan's Velveeta Recipe

INGREDIENTS

2 eggs
⅔ cup milk
¼ teaspoon salt
⅛ teaspoon paprika
1 cup macaroni (uncooked measure), cooked
    and drained
½ large bar of Velveeta
Bread crumbs
Butter

1. Preheat oven to 350° and butter a baking dish.
2. Beat eggs, milk, salt, and paprika together.
3. Pour a layer of cooked macaroni in baking dish.
4. Cover with a layer of Velveeta slices.
5. Add another layer of macaroni and then another layer of Velveeta. Continue layering.
6. Pour the egg-milk mixture over the top of the layers.
7. Sprinkle top with bread crumbs, dots of butter, and grated Velveeta.
8. Bake for 30 to 40 minutes.

Vicky's Macaroni and Cheese

INGREDIENTS

1½ cups macaroni (uncooked measure)
4 tablespoons butter
3 ounces cream cheese
8 ounces cheddar cheese, grated
1 cup sour cream
1 cup ricotta cheese
1 egg
Salt and pepper (to taste)
Paprika

1. Preheat oven to 350°.
2. Cook macaroni al dente. Drench in butter.
3. Soften cream cheese and mix with cheddar cheese, sour cream, ricotta, and egg. Add salt and pepper.

PLAIN JANE'S TIP
FOR DISGUISING FOOD:
Thoroughly wash and save cottage cheese containers. Fill them with vanilla ice cream and store in the freezer at your office. During lunch breaks, none of your co-workers will suspect you're not dieting.

4. Butter a baking dish and pour in macaroni.
5. Add the cheese mixture and sprinkle the top with paprika.
6. Bake for half an hour in a 350° oven or until browned.

GENERAL TIPS FOR MAKING YOUR FOOD MORE FATTENING

1) Deep-fry everything.

2) Always serve lots of bread and butter with each course.

3) Never read labels.

4) Serve huge portions.

5) Sprinkle coconut over everything.

6) Smother every dish with ketchup.

7) Use a lot of Velveeta.

8) Only prepare recipes that need a graham cracker crust.

9) Drink a lot of beer with your meals.

10) Eat at my mother's house.

Washington-to-New York Lasagna

ON a recent trip from Washington, D.C. to New York City, I decided to travel by train instead of plane. I enjoy taking the train for one important reason: the club car. Even though the train takes two hours longer than the plane, I think it is time well spent when I can be guzzling beer and munching pretzels.

On this particular trip, I was sitting next to Vicky, a colleague of mine who had attended the same Washington convention. We briefly discussed the convention before getting on to more serious business, namely, Vicky's recipe for la-

KITCHEN ETIQUETTE:

1) Be kind to your soufflé

2) Be nice to your Jello mold

3) Be mean with your greens

sagna. From Philadelphia to Penn Station, I wrote down the following recipe.

A few weeks later, I tested this recipe and, let me tell you, this makes a lot of lasagna. (This recipe will serve 15 to 18 people.) But don't cut down on the ingredients. It takes so much time and effort to make lasagna, you should always prepare two pans and either freeze the extra pan or invite some more friends to dinner.

Before you start cooking, make sure you have two lasagna pans. Vicky recommends buying the fluted porcelain variety but, listen to Plain Jane, and pick up disposable aluminum lasagna pans which have two great advantages: they're cheap and you never have to wash them.

Be forewarned that preparing this dish will involve using almost every dish, mixing bowl, pot, and pan in your pantry. I would not attempt this recipe without easy access to a dishwasher.

Because I hate to wash dishes, I usually avoid recipes that require so many utensils. However, as Vicky said while our train dashed by 125th Street, "If you really love lasagna, you learn to cope with tomato sauce splattered all over the wall."

INGREDIENTS

6 Italian sausages (3 sweet and 3 hot)
2 pounds ground chuck or lean beef
4 garlic cloves, chopped or pressed
2 28-ounce cans crushed & peeled tomatoes
1 15-ounce can tomato sauce
1 6-ounce can tomato paste
2 teaspoons sugar
Oregano
Salt and pepper
Basil
2 pounds fresh pasta (green or white) or 2 boxes lasagna noodles
Olive oil
3 pounds mozzarella cheese
3 pounds ricotta cheese
2 eggs
4 ounces Parmesan cheese, grated

1. To prepare the sauce, fry sausages in a small

amount of water and then brown until done.

2. In another frying pan, brown ground beef and garlic. Pour off any excess fat.

3. Cut cooked sausages into ½″ slices and put in a *large* saucepan. Add the browned beef.

4. Pour in the four cans of tomatoes. Add sugar, a generous amount of oregano, salt and pepper, and basil. Cook for about one hour, tasting and adjusting spices to your own particular palate.

5. Prepare lasagna. If you use fresh lasagna (which Vicky and I recommend) then you don't need to boil it. (Also, use whole sheets of fresh pasta instead of cutting into noodles.)

For boxed lasagna, put 2 tablespoons of olive oil in boiling water and then put in noodles, one at a time. Boil for about 10 to 12 minutes, stirring occasionally. Drain in colander and keep separated on a clean dishtowel.

6. Preheat oven to 350°.

7. Slice mozzarella and set aside.

8. Mix ricotta with eggs and set aside.

9. Spread a little sauce on the bottom of your pan and assemble layers of ingredients in the following order:

a layer of noodles

spread ricotta mixture over noodles with a spatula

sauce (blend with ricotta mixture)

mozzarella cheese

Parmesan cheese

10. Keep alternating layers and top with mozzarella and Parmesan cheeses.

11. Put aluminum pans on a cookie sheet (easier to lift) and place in a 350° oven for 45 to 60 minutes.

12. Serve with extra, heated sauce.

Like most great cheese and pasta dishes, this one gets better and better every time it's reheated. Vicky said to remind you that this dish takes a while to reheat since it is so dense.

You'll have lots of leftover sauce, which you should save for almost any other pasta dish.

Washington-to-New York Lasagna can easily be frozen and stored in your freezer.

Eggplant Parmigiana with Smoked Mozzarella

I don't like to brag (well, actually, I don't mind) but it is true that I, personally, invented this recipe for Eggplant Parmigiana (E.P., for short).

There are two secrets to this dish. One, you must use *smoked* mozzarella, which you can find in most Italian delicatessens. (I know it's a pain in the neck to make a special trip just for the cheese, but bear with me here. If this book does nothing else except turn you on to smoked mozzarella, then it's well worth its cover price.)

The second secret is that I don't fry the eggplant in olive oil—I broil it in the oven. Oh, I know that I will be accused of creating a somewhat dietetic dish but, believe me, that was *never* my intention. Originally, I merely wanted to eliminate that bread-crumb taste in most E.P. dishes. (I'm somewhat of an expert in this area as E.P. was my most-often ordered dinner in an Italian restaurant and, most of the time, it was awful. Of course, now that I make it so perfectly, I don't have to order it anymore)

Aside from potatoes, eggplant is the one vegetable that I really, really like. And this dish is very special because you actually get to taste the eggplant (not the bread crumbs) and this fabulous cheese.

If you make this dish for company then, by all means, take credit for cooking in the low-calorie method. Do not, however, tell your guests about all the extra cheese that's loaded into this dish to compensate for the loss of calories.

INGREDIENTS

4 or 5 eggplants (medium size)
1 large package mozzarella cheese
1 large smoked mozzarella cheese
1 jar Aunt Millie's Meatless Spaghetti Sauce
Parmesan cheese
Basil (fresh, if available, or dried)
Oregano

1. Peel eggplant and slice thin (about ⅛-inch to ¼-inch).

2. Cover cookie sheet (or aluminum broiler pan) with a layer of eggplant slices. Place under the broiler for a few minutes (just before eggplant starts to brown).

3. Turn slices and broil on other side. Continue broiling slices while you put together the casserole.
4. Slice the mozzarella cheeses by hand or processor.
5. Cover the bottom of a large, oven-proof casserole with some of the sauce.
6. Turn the oven down to 350° when removing the eggplant. Put a layer of the broiled eggplant slices over the sauce. Dot with a little more sauce on top of eggplant.
7. Add a layer of the mozzarella cheese, combining both the plain and the smoked.
8. Sprinkle with Parmesan cheese, basil, and oregano.
9. Add a little more sauce.
10. Add another layer of the eggplant.
11. Dot with sauce, add mozzarella cheeses, spices, and Parmesan.
12. Continue alternating layers until the top of the casserole. End with a layer of mozzarella coated with sauce and sprinkled with spices and Parmesan. (If you run out of room in the casserole and still have plenty of the ingredients left over, then start another casserole and freeze it for later use.)
13. Bake in a 350° oven for about 1 hour or until browned and bubbly.

Dear Plain Jane,
   Of the nine cooking methods—boiling, steaming, pressure-cooking, braising, roasting, broiling, microwave, pan-frying, and deep-frying—which do you recommend for preparing chicken?
Diana L.
Shreveport, La.

Dear Miss Show-Off from Shreveport,
   I'm not impressed by the rather obvious way you flaunt your cooking knowledge. Nine methods, indeed!
   Who's the expert here, you or me?
   If you're so darned smart, go fix your own chicken.
Jane

   P.S. What's braising?

Plain Jane
Pesto for Pasta

EXCEPT for getting into a bathing suit, I love summer. Summer means basil is in bloom and basil means pesto.

Here's my simpliest pesto recipe. Use this amount for one pound of linguine.

INGREDIENTS

2 cups fresh basil leaves
½ cup olive oil
1 clove garlic
½ teaspoon salt
3 tablespoons soft butter
½ cup fresh Parmesan cheese, grated

1. In blender, combine basil, olive oil, garlic, and salt.
2. Beat in butter and cheese.
3. Cook 1 pound linguine and toss with pesto sauce.

PLAIN JANE'S DOS AND DONT'S
When Eating in Front of the TV . . .

DON'T watch the Six O'Clock News while eating dinner.
DO watch M*A*S*H re-runs.

DON'T watch the Dukes of Hazzard, Love Boat or any show with Richard Dawson on a full stomach.

DON'T get mad during the commercial breaks.
DO get Haagen Dazs.

DON'T cook while watching Julia Child.
DO eat Mallomars.

DON'T watch TV, eat dinner, yell at your kids and read the newspaper at the same time.
DO save the newspaper until after you eat.

DON'T eat spaghetti with tomato sauce while watching an engrossing movie.
DO eat Spaghetti-O's.

Dear Plain Jane,
What can I do when my children insist on eating pretzels and potato chips before dinner? How can I stop them from spoiling their appetites?

Concerned Mom
St. Paul, Minnesota

Dear Mom in Minnesota,
I don't inderstand your question. What does "spoiling their appetites" mean? I've heard this is a state where one doesn't want to eat but, personally, I've never really experienced such a sensation. In fact, my appetite is the one totally *unspoiled* territory on my anatomy.

Since I've never fully grasped this particular concept, I do not feel qualified to answer your query. Perhaps Dear Abby could help . . . .

So sorry,
Jane

P.S. At my house pretzels and potato chips are the perfect appetizer, so I'm double confused by your letter.

Plain Jane Pasta Cream Sauce

PASTA is most fattening when served with a cream sauce. This one is a real killer because it's so easy to make that your only excuse not to make it is if you're out of heavy cream.

INGREDIENTS

1½ cups sweet heavy cream
½ stick sweet butter
½ teaspoon salt
¾ cup fresh grated Parmesan cheese
1½ cups chopped fresh parsley and chives

1. In a saucepan, combine cream, butter, and salt. Stir over heat until reduced and thickened.
2. Blend in cheese and herbs.
3. Simmer until ready to serve but stir often to avoid sticking to pan.

Serve over a pound of thin spaghetti or any pasta of your choice. (By the way, this recipe is worth a special trip to the market for a container of heavy cream.)

Side Dishes

A great side dish can make all the difference between an almost-dietetic and a really fattening meal.

If you have any doubts about the caloric content of your next meal, simply prepare one of the side dishes in this chapter and rest assured that your dinner will far exceed the required 13,000 calorie mark. Boston Baked Beans and Lynn's Potato Casserole are particularly effective in transforming borderline Weight Watcher dinners into Plain Jane feasts.

Keep in mind that side dishes can also be served as entrées. For example, Fresh-Baked Bread (with lots of sweet butter) makes the perfect main course.

Fresh-Baked Bread

Caramelized Sweet Potatoes with Chestnuts

Lynn's Potato Casserole

Plain Jane's One and Only Money-Saving Recipe

Do the Mashed Potato

Baked Potato

Potato Kugel with Zucchini and Carrots

Homemade Pasta

My Dentist's Receptionist's Zucchini Casserole

Spinach and Cheese Casserole

Ketchup: A Meal in Itself?

Harriet's Crunchy Macaroni Salad

Boston Baked Beans

Best Mayo Recipe

Fresh-Baked Bread

IS there anything more aromatic than fresh-baked bread? I never knew about the intoxicating delight of such a fragrance until I had dinner one night at my friend Ella's house.

Ella learned to bake bread as a defense tactic when she lived, for three years, in the Midwest where she couldn't buy anything other than Wonder Bread.

My favorite dinner with Ella consisted of three loaves of fresh-baked French bread and two bottles of wine. We baked the bread together. Ella did all kinds of funny things with the yeast, kneaded the dough until her face turned blue and then cleaned up the floury mess that covered the kitchen counter and floor. I drank the wine, commented repeatedly on how hard it was to bake bread, and played War with Sarah, Ella's daughter.

I concluded from this episode that baking bread at home was simply too much work. True, the bread was delicious. But there's a fabulous Italian bakery not two blocks from my house, where Zito bakes fresh bread that's every bit as good as homemade.

So, my advice is simple. Buy your bread at Zito's and pop it in the oven for a minute or two for that "warm-from-the-oven" fragrance.

If, however, you live in a town where there isn't a decent bakery for miles, do what Ella did. Move.

PLAIN JANE'S DOS AND DON'TS
At the Supermarket . . .

DON'T eat the Entenmann's before checking out at the cash register.
DO go for the Reese's Pieces (much less messy to eat).

DON'T fight over the last box of Mallomars.
DO cry.

DON'T take the Honda Civic to the market for shopping.
DO take the eighteen-wheeler.

DON'T take the children along when you food-shop.
DO take a knife and fork.

Caramelized Sweet Potatoes with Chestnuts

I used to think I didn't like sweet potatoes because I never ate the sweet potato pie at Thanksgiving. It did seem very odd to me that there was actually a fattening food I didn't like.

Sure enough, it turns out that I love sweet potatoes but hate pineapple. Don't get me wrong, I love fresh pineapple—I'm just not really fond of it in hot food.

If you, or anyone in your family, has had a similar experience and you find a mountain of sweet potato pie left over the day after Thanksgiving, then try the following recipe for sweet potatoes and chestnuts.

INGREDIENTS

Remember that it's redundant to eat junk food while watching television.

3 *pounds sweet potatoes*
3 *apples*
¼ *cup lemon juice*
1 *10-ounce can whole chestnuts (packed in water)*
½ *cup brown sugar*
½ *cup sweet butter*
½ *cup honey*
½ *teaspoon cinnamon*
¼ *teaspoon ginger*

1. Boil sweet potatoes until tender but firm.
2. While the potatoes cool, peel, core, and slice apples. Toss apples with lemon juice.
3. Peel and slice sweet potatoes and arrange them with the apples and the chestnuts in a shallow, buttered baking dish. Preheat the oven to 400°.
4. In a separate saucepan, stir the sugar, butter, honey, cinnamon, and ginger and cook over moderate heat. Stir constantly until sugar dissolves.
5. Spoon sugar mixture over the potatoes, apples, and chestnuts.
6. Bake in a 400° oven, basting once or twice, for half an hour or until brown and bubbly.

This recipe will serve 10 people as a side dish.

Lynn's Potato Casserole

HERE'S my favorite story about my friend Lynn. When she divorced her husband (whom I told her not to marry when we were still in high school), she didn't know what to do with their old wedding picture. She simply looked too terrific in her wedding gown to throw the picture away and she wasn't about to ruin it with a pair of scissors. So, instead, she found a photograph of Tom Selleck and pasted Tom's face over her ex-husband's.

Equally creative in the kitchen, Lynn fondly remembers this potato casserole as a favorite from those days when cooking took up a major portion of her time.

INGREDIENTS

6 *medium-sized potatoes, cooked and sliced*
2 *cups creamed cottage cheese*
2 *tablespoons melted butter*
2 *tablespoons flour*
1 *teaspoon salt*
2 *tablespoons chopped chives*
¼ *teaspoon black pepper*
½ *teaspoon thyme*
⅓ *cup milk*
½ *cup bread crumbs (buttered)*
2 *tablespoons Parmesan cheese*
Butter

1. Preheat oven to 350°.
2. In a greased, 1½-quart casserole, place a layer of the cooked and sliced potatoes.
3. In a separate bowl, beat together the cottage cheese and melted butter. Spread a layer of this over the potatoes.
4. Combine the flour, salt, chives, pepper, and thyme and sprinkle some of the mixture over the cottage cheese.
5. Repeat alternate layers, ending with potatoes.
6. Pour milk over everything.
7. Combine bread crumbs and Parmesan cheese and sprinkle over casserole.
8. Dot with butter and bake for 30 minutes.

FIVE GUARANTEED WEIGHT LOSS TECHNIQUES:*

1) Keep your mouth shut

2) Stop licking your plate clean

3) Don't finish dessert

4) Get up from the table after the appetizer

5) Destroy your McDonald's charge card

*Untested by Plain Jane

Plain Jane's One and Only Money-Saving Recipe

EVERY time you peel potatoes, thoroughly wash the potatoes before peeling, then save the peels in a plastic bag stored in your freezer. When you have a cup of skins, combine them with 2 tablespoons of melted butter, bread crumbs, and grated Parmesan cheese. Put the breaded skins on a baking sheet and broil for three minutes.

Do The Mashed Potato

WHEN preparing mashed potatoes, fold in a good quantity of grated cheddar cheese and sour cream. Put into a casserole, sprinkle with paprika, and bake in a 350° oven for 15 minutes or until browned and piping hot.

Baked Potato

ALWAYS coat the skin of a potato with melted butter before baking. Bake for half an hour in a hot oven, pierce the potato with a fork and let it bake for another half hour.

Potato Kugel with Carrots and Zucchini

I think that *kugel* means "pudding." I know that any time you see the word, you can bet a fattening recipe will follow. This is a case in point.

Mom makes this kugel with carrots and zucchini but, I promise, you'll never know the vegetables are there.

INGREDIENTS

12 ounces grated potatoes
1 cup grated zucchini
1 cup grated carrots
4 eggs, slightly beaten
2 ounces diced onions
¼ cup matzoh meal or flour
1 tablespoon plus 1 teaspoon vegetable oil
¼ teaspoon salt
White pepper

1. Preheat oven to 375°.
2. Strain grated potato and squeeze off all excess

water. Transfer to a bowl.
3. Do the same with the zucchini. Add to potatoes. Add carrots.
4. Add eggs, onions, matzoh meal, and oil. Stir.
5. Season with salt and pepper.
6. Put mixture in a greased 2-quart casserole dish and bake in a preheated 375° oven for 45 minutes or until well browned.

Mom says you can also bake this kugel in individual tin muffin cups for separate portions. Serve warm with plenty of applesauce.

Homemade Pasta

TODAY there is a proliferation of pasta-making machines.

For my general advice on homemade pasta, see my instructions on fresh-baked bread (pg. 105).

Dear Plain Jane,
Last night I woke up and found, to my horror, that I was standing in front of the refrigerator.
I don't know how I got to the kitchen or why I was eating a fistful of maple walnut ice cream. What's happening to me?
Fern M.
Forest Hills, N.Y.

Dear Fern,
Don't panic. You are merely suffering from a common sleep disorder called Sleep Eating.
Yours is a mild case. People have been known to wake up and find themselves at their nearest Burger King. (The next time you're in a local fast-food restaurant late at night, see if you can spot the people who are actually in the deep recesses of Sleep Eating.)
I wouldn't worry about this problem; I'm sure it will pass. However, I do advise you *not* to buy any more maple walnut ice cream. Even fast asleep, I'd rather be eating chocolate fudge swirl.
Jane

My Dentist's Receptionist's Zucchini Casserole

EDIE is my dentist's receptionist and my dentist is also my brother-in-law.

I often hear from Edie because she's always sending little postcards reminding me that it's been a very long time since my last check-up. (Edie, I promise to come in as soon as I'm done with this manuscript.)

Last year, Edie gave this recipe to my sister (the dentist's wife) and my sister gave it to me.

Considering Edie was working with zucchini, she did wonders with this recipe. Unless someone told you, you'd never guess that there was a vegetable buried underneath all of this stuffing and sour cream.

INGREDIENTS

4 cups zucchini
2 carrots, shredded
1 small onion, grated
1 can cream of chicken soup
½ cup sour cream
1 6- or 8-ounce package stuffing (Edie uses Pepperidge Farm Herb Seasoned Stuffing)
⅓ cup melted butter

1. Preheat oven to 350°.
2. Slice zucchini and cook, briefly, in water.
3. Drain and combine with carrots and onion.
4. Add soup and sour cream.
5. Separately, mix stuffing with butter. (Edie uses a bit more than ⅓ cup; she keeps adding butter until stuffing is moist.)
6. Add half the stuffing to vegetable mixture.
7. Pour into a 2-quart casserole and top with the remaining stuffing.
8. Bake for 25 minutes in 350° oven.

Spinach and Cheese Casserole

2 packages frozen leaf spinach
2 eggs
1½ pounds of cheese, combination of mozzarella, Jarlsberg, and Swiss (or your choice of cheeses), cubed

1. Preheat oven to 350°.
2. Cook spinach as directed on package.

3. Put in small casserole and add beaten eggs.

4. Put in cubes of cheese. Combine whatever cheeses you most like.

5. Bake at 350° for 40 minutes or until cheese bubbles and top browns.

KETCHUP is the ultimate food substance for people of all ages.

If you are under 12 years old, it is permissible to use ketchup with everything you eat from eggs to hot dogs.

During your lean years, ketchup will serve as a substitute for the real food you can't afford. (Ketchup and water is the traditional soup course for all starving artists.)

As a parent, you can sneak a dollop of ketchup from your child's plate every time you feel virtuous enough to personally abstain from using this high-calorie condiment.

In your old age, you can slip back into the eating habits of a nine-year-old and blame creeping senility for your unhealthy tendencies.

Ketchup: A Meal In Itself?

Dear Plain Jane,
How long does it take for water to boil?

Robin M.
Salem, Mass.

Dear Robin,
That depends on what you're boiling it *for*.

If you are in a hurry to boil up some hot dogs for your kids, it will take approximately forever.

If, however, you put the pot on the stove before jumping into a quick shower, it'll take one split second to boil (and two seconds to boil over.)

Jane

Dear Plain Jane,
What is clotted cream?

Selma S.
Cincinnati, Ohio

Dear Selma,
Don't ask.

Jane

Harriet's Crunchy Macaroni Salad

COMBINE a box of cooked macaroni, red pepper, green pepper, radishes, lots of mayo, salt, pepper, paprika, and celery salt (to taste.) Add an extra dollop of mayo every time you serve Harriet's salad.

Dear Plain Jane,
  I'm always hungry and I love to eat.
How do you know when to stop eating?

Sylvia
Chicago, Ill.

Dear Sylvia,
  If I knew how to answer your question, I wouldn't be 15 pounds overweight . . . now would I?

Jane

Boston Baked Beans

I literally went all the way to Boston to get an authentic baked bean recipe. Well, okay, not Boston but Medford, a suburb of Boston. Close enough. And these beans are close enough to perfection to be well worth the trip.

Boston Baked Beans are easy to make but they require a lot of time and some watching. But believe me, this recipe will change your opinion of baked beans as merely an accessory for frankfurters.

Sound New Englander advice from Aunt Fran in Medford is to double this recipe and freeze the remainder for another time. (Leftover beans will be a little mushy but they'll taste great.)

INGREDIENTS

1 pound dry beans (preferably lima beans, but you can use small pea beans)
1 whole peeled onion
Chunk of fat or fat brisket
½ cup dark brown sugar
¼ cup molasses
2 teaspoons dry mustard
1 tablespoon salt
Pepper (a few shakes)
Ketchup (a few shakes)

1. Place beans in a large pot and cover with water. Use generous amount of water because beans will absorb much of the liquid. Soak overnight.
2. Preheat oven to 300°.
3. After soaking, pour off excess water; leave just enough to cover beans.
4. Add all the other ingredients.
5. Bake in a covered pot at 300° until tender. Stir occasionally.
6. Remove cover after an hour or two so beans will get browner and liquid will reduce. If beans get too brown, replace cover. If they get too dry, add water and cover again.
7. It will take several hours for beans to be tender, so plan on cooking them between 4 and 6 hours.

Open the Hellmann's.

(I've tasted lots of homemade mayonnaise and it's never any better than the bottled kind. And talk about a lot of work! Mayo is harder to make than baklava.)

Best Mayo Recipe

PLAIN JANE'S DOS AND DON'TS
At the buffet table . . .

DON'T put more food on your plate than you can carry with two hands.
DO ask a waiter to help carry your desserts back to your table.

DON'T pile your plate higher than 3½ inches.
DO take two plates if necessary.

DON'T stuff a 10-pound roast beef into your evening purse.
DO ask for a doggie bag.

DON'T spend the entire evening eating at your table.
DO circulate to other tables, eat one plateful, and then move on to another table with another full plate.

Appendix

Cooking Schools
(MANHATTAN LISTINGS):

The High School of Performing Chefs
Grades 9–12
High-school seniors learn to prepare a soufflé
while tap dancing like Fred Astaire. Girls are
taught to dance backwards. 765 West 53rd St.,
New York, N.Y. 10066

Junior Pizza Academy
Grades 7–10
Middle grades incorporating principles of New
Math, Old English, and Deep Dish Individual
Pizzas. Students graduate to large pies and box
folding. Optional courses: Anchovies, Pepperoni,
and Sausage. Affiliated with several pizzerias
in the Tri-state area. 23400 Carmine Street, Little Italy, New York, New York 12222.

Yeshiva Gourmet
Boys to age 13
Boys are trained in the Talmud and in preparations for their bar mitzvah brunch. Courses include latke frying, buying lox in quantity, and
sculpturing in chicken livers. 37 LeKiyem Rd.,
Brooklyn, N.Y. 19999

The Little Red Kitchen
Grade K–6
Children are drilled in the basics of reading,
writing, 'rithmetic, and Ragu. Morning and
afternoon sessions. No alcoholic beverages are
served until parents arrive. 1967 Bleecker Street,
Greenwich Village, N.Y. 35576.

The Dieter's Computer Gourmet Cooking Tennis Camp
Overweight girls 4 months to 37 years
Girls are taught to play tennis on their computers while preparing low calorie, gourmet meals in a microwave oven. Professional guidance for addictions to Tab and Sweet 'N' Low. Optional courses in buying wholesale, ripping sweatshirts, and fading your Calvin Kleins. Located in the heart of the Catskills, Loch Sheldrake, N.Y. 99999.

A Glossary of Gourmet Terms

Throughout *Plain Jane's Thrill of Very Fattening Foods Cookbook* I have used technical terms from the multilingual art of cooking. As a service to my readers, I have compiled the following glossary in order to explain the more complicated language used in this book.

Al Dente: A dessert that is so sweet, it makes your teeth tingle.

Ale: Ale, the gang's all here!

Almond Paste: Better to sniff than Elmer's Glue.

Amandine: The proper dressing for any low calorie entree.

Anchovy: What you hold when ordering the pizza.

Antipasto: Not spaghetti.

Aperitif: Important.

Aspic: A place to ski.

Au Naturel: Without much flavor.

Bean Curd: What you never order for lunch.

Beer: What you always order for lunch.

Blanch: DuBois.

Brioche: Fancy Parker House rolls.

Broth: Liquid bouillon cube.

Calorie: Something to ignore.

Carbohydrates: The only reason to run in a marathon.

Caviar: Very expensive sodium.

Chips: Erik Estrada.

Chocolate: If you don't know the meaning of this word, I don't want you reading my book.

Clarified Butter: The opposite of misunderstood margarine.

Coddle: To pet a fish.

Measurement Equivalents

Consommé: Very diluted Campbell's.

2 tablespoons	=	1 fluid ounce
4 tablespoons	=	¼ cup
16 tablespoons	=	1 cup
16 candles	=	Sweet 16 party
1 cup	=	½ pint
½ pint	=	Napoleon
2 cups	=	1 bra
1 pint	=	16 ounces
1 quart	=	2 pints
1 gallon	=	8 miles (HWY)

Cornstarch: What you use to iron the vegetables.

Cream of Tartar: The best of nicotine-nicotine.

Croissant: Difficult to pronounce.

Crudités: Uncouth vegetables.

Crumb: My ex-boyfriend.

Crumpet: My ex-boyfriend's son.

Crustacean: My ex-boyfriend's father.

Decant: So Ruby will.

Deep-fat Frying: The best method for cooking food.

Deglaze: Remove de glaze.

Demi-glaze: A little bit glazed.

Demitasse: Half tassed.

Dice: Your odds are better with Blackjack.

Dilute: Midwestern way to make gravy.

Dip: Fancy dance step.

Doughnuts: Breakfast.

Drawn Butter: Very similar to illustrated Crisco.

Dredge: To talk about old diets.

Dumpling: Yes, sweetie pie.

Dutch Oven: Range that pays for itself.

Entree: Come in.

Metric Conversions

LIQUID MEASURES

1 tablespoon	=	¼ deciliter		
½ cup	=	1 deciliter		
1 cup	=	¼ liter		
2 cups	=	1 pint	=	½ liter
4 cups	=	32 ounces	=	1 liter
4 cups	=	on sidewalk	=	1 liter bug

Espresso: The Italian postal service.

Filet Mignon: See *Croissant*.

Florentine: Henderson, the Wesson Oil Lady.

Fritter: Doing nothing in the kitchen but eating potato chips.

Garnish: The stuff you don't eat.

Gherkin: Distant relative of the Munchkin.

Giblets: The yucky stuff.

Grappa: Lives with Gramma.

Grate: Robert Redford.

Gravlax: Serious salmon.

Grease: A movie.

Griddle: Dee-dee and La-dee-da.

Grill: Ask lots of personal questions.

Head Cheese: Don't know. Don't want to know.

Hip: Where you find the cellulite.

Hors d'Oeuvres: French equivalent of potato chips, pretzels, peanuts, and aerosol cheese.

Humble Pie: Not nearly as tasty as apple or blueberry.

Hush Puppies: Shush, dogs!

Jelly: The Plain Jane way to eat strawberries.

Julienne: Bond.

Kettle: Ma and Pa.

Knead: Not what you want, what you get.

Metric Conversions

SOLID MEASURES

1 ounce	=	30 grams		
4 ounces	=	¼ pound	=	115 grams
8 ounces	=	½ pound	=	225 grams
1 Michael Jackson	=	11 Grammies		
16 ounces	=	1 pound	=	450 grams
36 ounces	=	1 kilogram		
60 letters	=	air mail	=	1 telegram

Ladyfingers: Manicured cookies.

Lager: Guy who cuts down trees.

Langouste: See *Foie Gras*.

Lard: Give us this day our daily bread.

Lazy Susan: My sister, sometimes.

Laurel: and Hardy.

Leaven: Worth.

Lox: Keeps out burglars.

Temperatures

FAHRENHEIT				CELSIUS/CENTIGRADE
	32	water freezes	0	
	212	water boils	100	
	300–325	low oven	149–163	
	400–425	hot oven	204–218	
	500–525	extremely hot oven	260–274	
	575–600	kiss dinner goodbye	314–319	
	625–700	kiss kitchen goodbye	364–439	

Magnum: P.I.

Mango: Woman stay.

Margarine: My Little, an Italian TV show now in syndication.

Marrow: Edward R., famed newscaster.

Mash: Television show.

Mayonnaise: The most important jar in your refrigerator.

Melba Toast: Substance unknown to Plain Jane.

Microwave Oven: Not the place to dry the French poodle.

Minute Steak: The amount of time it takes to eat dinner.

Mixed Grill: Being asked personal questions by both your father and your mother.

Muffin: Nickname for rich girls who live in Connecticut.

Mush: Aftermash.

Nouvelle Cuisine: Not enough to eat.

Parfait: The course.

Parsley: Sage, rosemary, and thyme.

Pasta: Imperative at least once a day.

Pastrami: Italian inventor of pasteurized milk.

Poach: To steal food from your dinner companion's plate.

Popover: To visit a friend.

Prune: Clean out your refrigerator by eating everything in it.

Puff Pastry: Dragon cookie.

Puree: Opposite of polluted A.

Quail: Anorexic chicken.

Quiche: A fattening way to cook spinach.

Relish: Enjoy eating.

Saccharin: Early version of Sweet N' Low.

Sake: Japanese Double Martini.

Scald: To punish the milk.

Scallion: An anorexic onion.

Sugar Boiling Temperatures

	F	C
Soft Ball	237	114
Hard Ball	247	119
Ball Four	You're	Out
Soft Crack	280	140
Hard Crack	310	154
Caramel	340	171

Scampi: Where Italians send their children for the summer.

Sear: The place to buy Cheryl Tiegs's sportswear.

Shad: Used to sing with Jeremy.

Sherbet: Almost ice cream.

Shortbread: Serve with tall butter.

Shortening: Opposite of longing.

Shred: and Ethel Mertz.

Sift: Get cramps in your hand.

Simmer: Time, and the living is easy.

Smorgasbord: Everybody overeats.

Soufflé: Don't bother me.

Squab: Fight among fowls.

Steam: To remove wrinkles from clothes or flavor from food.

Tabasco: Italian diet soda.

Tahini: Where Gauguin painted.

Tamale: I'll think about it.

Toddy: Hot senator from Massachusetts.

Tofu: See *Bean Curd*.

Vermicelli: Italian lice.

Vermouth: State that borders on Massachusetts and New Hampshire.

Veronique: Went to high school with Archie and Betty.

Waffle: Can't decide what to order for dinner.

Water Chestnut: Not good for roasting on an open fire.

Wok: What you do from 9 to 5.

Wurst: Victoria Principal in a leotard.

Recommended Reading

Dr. Hoss Cartwright, *Eat to Win/Cook to Get Rained Out*.

Jacques Cousteau & Pepin, *La Technique of Cooking Underwater*.

Fannie Farmer, *The Farmer in the Dill*.

Mad Hatter, *The Mad Hatter Book of Great Cheshire Desserts*.

Jerry & Ethan Jones, *Book of Bread: 101 Ways to Make Money*.

Julia Kid, *A Kid's Kitchen: Mastering the Fine Art of French Fingerpainting*.

James Mustache, *Mustache on Pasta: Removing Hair From Italian Food*.

Peter Pan, *The Captain Hook Complex: Biting the Hand That Feeds You*.

Waverley Root, *Silly Names for Your Baby*.

Dinah Shore, *How to Cook a Chevrolet*.

Martha Hungarian Stew, *Cooking Quick with Zsa Zsa; Entertaining with Eva*.

Index

**An Open Letter
to My Readers**

Dear Reader,

There's an empty page at the end of this book
for two reasons:
1) I wanted to provide my readers with space
for emergency phone numbers, and
2) I have run out of recipes.

The material in this book has depleted all of
the good recipes from the files of my family and
my friends. Quite simply, I have run out of people to call. (Well, I do have a few really distant relatives I could call, but that would be asking
an awful lot of me.)

So, here's the situation—I don't have any material left over for the sequel: *Plain Jane's Thrill
of MORE Very Fattening Foods Cookbook*.

I've thought a lot about this and, frankly, I
think it's only fair that you, my readers, provide
me with enough recipes for another book. After all, I've sacrificed a lot for you. I've given you
the best recipes of my life. I've cajoled recipes
from friends and family I wouldn't otherwise call
for all the tea in China. And now, I honestly
feel that the least I deserve in return is one lousy
recipe from you.

So, send me your best recipe. It has to be one
of your originals, not one that you've copied
from another cookbook. Send it to me in care of
my publisher: St. Martin's Press, 175 Fifth
Avenue, New York, N.Y. 10010, and we'll call
ourselves even.

If your recipe tests out in my kitchen, I'll include it in my next book. I won't pay you a
dime (I didn't pay my closest friends, why should
I pay a total stranger?) but, in the book, I will
try to mention your name and, if possible, to spell
it correctly.

I could promise to send you a complimentary

copy of *MORE Very Fattening Foods Cookbook* but I'll probably forget to mail it and then you'll be bitterly disappointed. (Well, that's the way it is when you're dealing with famous writers, so it's better to prepare yourself beforehand.)

So, I'll look forward to hearing from you. And, please, don't take forever to find that stamp; I work under pretty tight deadlines, you know.

Love & Hershey Kisses,

Emergency
Phone Numbers

Pizzeria:_____

Carvel:_____

Chinese restaurant:_____

Supermarket:_____

Deli:_____

Liquor store:_____

Bakery:_____

Butcher:_____